How to Plan and Build
Fireplaces

By the Editors of Sunset Books and Sunset Magazine

Lane Publishing Co., Menlo Park, California

Warmth for the soul...and the body, too

Despite the widespread use of fossil-fueled and electric heating systems, the open hearth is so ingrained in our heritage as to be still a highly desirable feature in a home. Fireplaces fulfill our primal desire for the company of open flame, and we continue to build, use, and revere them as the home's focal point. But the conviction that a fireplace should warm more than the soul has prompted development of designs that are more efficient as heaters.

For those planning a new fireplace, this book emphasizes modern heat-circulating fireplaces and efficient fireplace design and placement. For those seeking to boost the heat of an existing fireplace, there are suggestions for adding heat-recovery devices. Also included are tips on fireplace use and maintenance, a chapter on wood stoves, and 48 pages of color photographs showing attractive fireplace designs.

We are grateful to the homeowners who opened their hearths to us for photographs. Warm thanks, also, to the following people for their many contributions: Obie Bowman; Mark Brown, Cricklewood Fireplace Shoppe; Buff & Hensman, A.I.A.; Anne De Wolf, The Golden Flame; Barbara DiConza; Judy Frost; Judy Giggy, Pajaro Dunes Rental Agency; Bob and Diana Halderman; Gail Holmes; Kala Point Development Co.; Bill Keller, House of Fireplaces; Ralph Kerr; Dan Lieberman; Mark Mills; Mark Nelson; Dick Queirolo; Ram's Head Rentals; Mark V. Sheehan, Fireplace Distributors of California; Robyn Shotwell Metcalfe; Jean Siegfried; David Smith; Donald W. Vandervort.

Staff Editors:

Jim Barrett
Kathryn L. Arthurs
Scott Fitzgerrell

Design: Robert Hu
Illustrations: Joe Seney

Cover: This circulating fireplace doubles as a supplementary heater. The raised concrete hearth supports a prefabricated metal firebox. At lower left, bricks were omitted to provide for one of two air intakes. Extended hearth offers seating and forms base for wood storage box. Architect: George Cody. Photograph by Steve W. Marley.

Editor, Sunset Books: David E. Clark

Fourth printing August 1984

CONTENTS

PLANNING FUNDAMENTALS

In this era of ever scarcer fuels, the fireplace is seen more and more as a practical heater. This is as it should be, but romanticists need not lose heart. An efficient fireplace can warm the soul as well as the toes, can spark warm friendships by drawing guests within its cheery circle, and can reflect the style of its owners. How? Because—although inner workings are what make or break a fireplace as a heater—efficiency can be masked behind the most pleasing face your imagination sees.

A fireplace evokes dozens, if not hundreds, of pleasing associations. Some come from as far back as when knights gathered in the great hall at Camelot. Some come from great movies—the big hearth in the grandfather's chalet in *Heidi* comes first to mind, but the one at the inn in *Tom Jones* wasn't bad, either. The best ones come from personal experience… Christmas mornings in childhood…a ski cabin with a foot of new powder gathering outside…a beach house with wind howling in the eaves and plenty of good books at hand.

The picture of the fireplace is almost as varied as the number of recollections, ranging from cavernous maw at Camelot to delicately carved Italian marble in a fine mansion to glow-in-the-dark orange metal pumpkin suspended in midair in an A-frame. But mostly the picture is of homey red brick supporting the kind of mantel that looks right with a row of Christmas stockings hanging from it.

The pictures are all perfect, but the real experiences may fall short, as most of us have learned from one heatless fire or another. The plain fact is that to earn its keep in almost any house, a fireplace must warm body as well as soul. Warmth for the soul is the easier kind; the physical heat of a fire is harder to come by, depending as it does solely on efficient design. As fossil fuels grow scarcer and their prices soar, usable heat becomes more and more the point of building a fireplace into a house. For many people, this means a new approach to planning what can—at its best—be only a supplementary source of warmth.

Much of the fun of choosing or designing a fireplace has long rested with its social warmth, its appearance. It still does. However, the serious questions of planners increasingly deal with heat efficiency. The pretty face comes *after* they develop a working base. For this reason, the planning text that follows focuses on heat efficiency. Further, in our gallery of successful designs, we call special attention to heat-efficient designs through use of this symbol: € HEAT EFFICIENT

How fireplaces heat

In terms of the way they heat, there are only three basic fireplaces:
- Conventional, almost always thought of as the good old brick fireplace with the kind of flue Santa comes down on Christmas Eve.
- Circulating, which adds, to the conventional design, a ducting system to transport fire-warmed air.
- Freestanding, most often thought of as a modern metal unit with many kinships to a wood-burning stove.

Conventional fireplaces

Though the conventional fireplace is all the same in many minds as a brick fireplace, masonry is not the only possibility. Prefabricated metal fireboxes and lightweight chimneys can be just as conventional in operation.

What makes a fireplace conventional is a solid firebox leading upward to a damper, smoke dome, smoke shelf, and chimney, as shown in the full-page drawing on page 8.

No matter what the material, the conventional fireplace is inefficient as a producer of heat. For all practical purposes, it gives off only radiant heat, and then mainly from the firebox opening—usually one side, rarely more than two.

Some refinements, built in or added on, can improve heat efficiency. Ducting outside air in to feed combustion reduces interior drafts caused by outside air rushing in through chinks in doors and windows to replace lost oxygen. (Some experts say that in a drafty house, a large blaze in a conventional fireplace can cause a net heat loss.) Conversely, in a weather-tight building, combustion air ducted from outside overcomes poor draw in a fireplace. In addition to ducting, heat-recovery devices and systems can be of help (see page 93).

Heat-circulating fireplaces

Heat-circulating fireplaces give off as much radiant heat as conventional types, but to this they add circulating air warmed by convection.

These fireplaces have a double or triple-wall firebox with an intervening airspace several inches wide. Vents at the bottom of the firebox draw cool air into this space between the inner and outer walls, where it is warmed. The heated air rises by convection to be expelled through vents located above the firebox opening, or farther away—even to other rooms—through ducts. In some models, small fans are installed inside the inlets to force more air around the firebox.

Heat-circulating fireplaces provide at least twice as much heat as well-designed conventional fireplaces.

A quick look back

First fireplaces were freestanding firepits roughly made of stone and located beneath the ridgepole so smoke could rise to maximum height before venting lazily through a hole in the roof. Hoods came much later.

Heat-circulating fireplaces were developed in the early 1700s. A French physician named Savot designed the earliest ones. Benjamin Franklin is responsible for the fit-in-a-fireplace Pennsylvania stove shown here; it was the first to duct outside air for combustion.

Fireplaces against walls first were responses to multistory medieval castles. They had to be huge to produce any heat at all; wall vents made them smoky. Modern dimensions did not come until Count Rumford designed efficient flues and firebox shapes during the 1700s.

Masonry fireplace styles

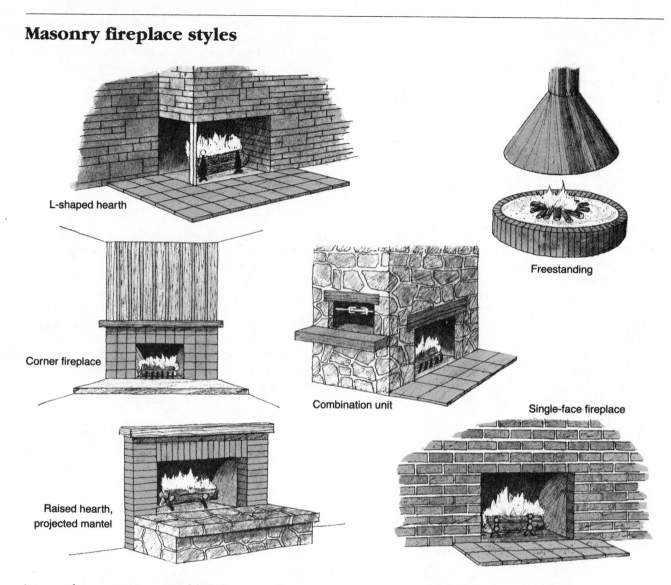

L-shaped hearth

Corner fireplace

Combination unit

Freestanding

Single-face fireplace

Raised hearth, projected mantel

As space heaters, conventional fireplaces are about 10 percent efficient—that is, 90 percent of the fire's heat goes up the flue. Circulating fireplaces are 25 to 30 percent efficient. As in the case of conventional fireplaces, their heat efficiency can be improved by combustion air ducted from outside. In addition, the option of ducting warmed air into an adjacent room makes them more versatile as well as more efficient.

Even at their best, though, heat-circulating fireplaces cannot be expected to provide more than supplemental heat in a house—sometimes in concert with a furnace, sometimes in place of one when only a modest amount of heat is needed to take the nip out of a chilly morning or evening in spring or autumn. A large model can serve as the primary heat source in a small cabin.

The majority of circulating fireplaces in use today are prefabricated metal units. Many are metal drop-ins in masonry fireplaces. A rare few are purely masonry designs.

Freestanding fireplaces

Freestanding fireplaces are fairly efficient heaters because they radiate to all sides. The type must be divided into at least two categories. One is the firepit, in which the fire is open to all sides, and in which smoke rises into a hood and then into a chimney. The other is the prefabricated metal unit, which typically is shaped somewhere between a cylinder and a sphere and has an opening on one side. A majority of these units are ultramodern in design.

Traditionalists have at least one option, though— the classic Franklin stove, which serves as a stove with its doors closed, a fireplace with them open. (A conventional masonry fireplace may be freestanding in the sense that it is an island set away from any wall; these units have some of the radiant efficiency of more typical freestanding units, but are not identically efficient.)

Freestanding fireplaces work best if located so heat

can radiate to all parts of a room. As with all other types, their efficiency is improved if combustion air can be ducted from outside, though this sometimes is difficult for remodelers to do, especially in the cases of slab floors or upper story installations.

Placing a fireplace in the middle of a room to gain the heat efficiency of a central location requires a tradeoff in the form of lost usable floor space. It can also make furniture location difficult.

How fireplaces are installed

Though the differences between the three basic fireplace types are important in planning, the choice is usually between masonry or prefabricated metal. These are the distinctions that count most; there is a world of difference in the way they are installed.

A masonry fireplace must be designed and built with professional skill; installing a prefabricated fireplace requires only basic carpentering techniques. Because of its great weight, not only must a masonry fireplace be built, it must be built from the ground up. A prefabricated fireplace, on the other hand, far from needing a foundation, is light enough to rest on standard flooring, so may be placed much more freely when added to an existing building. Finally, a masonry fireplace costs two to three times more than a prefabricated one. With these thoughts in mind, the following pages and the detailed installation chapters (starting on page 64) have been divided into

Designs in metal: Freestanding fireplaces

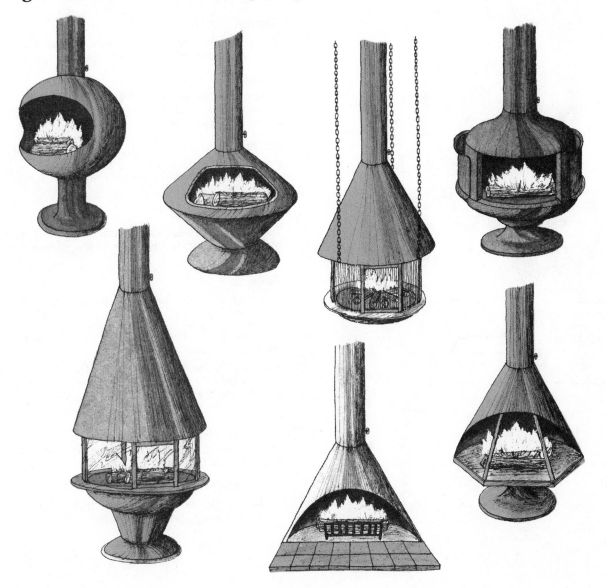

How a conventional fireplace works

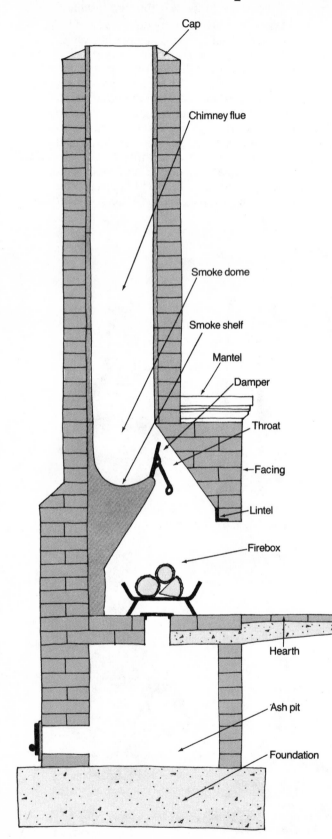

Chimney flue
Smoke and combustion gases from the burning wood pass up the chimney inside a flue, usually made of large-diameter terra cotta pipe or insulated steel.

Smoke dome
Acts as a funnel to compress smoke and gases rising from the fire so they will squeeze into the chimney flue above.

Smoke shelf
Bounces stray downdrafts back up the chimney before they can neutralize the updraft and blow smoke into the room.

Throat
Slotlike opening above the firebox, where flame, smoke, and combustion gases pass into the smoke chamber.

Damper
A steel or cast iron door that opens or closes the throat opening. Used to check and regulate draft, it prevents loss of heat up the chimney.

Lintel
Heavy steel brace that supports the masonry above the fireplace opening. Sometimes incorporated in the damper assembly.

Facing
Vertical surface around fireplace opening. May be built of various materials: brick, stone, concrete, tile, wood, metal.

Firebox
Chamber where the fire is built; made of steel or firebrick. Walls and back are slanted slightly to radiate heat into the room.

Hearth
Inner hearth of firebrick or steel holds the burning fuel; outer hearth of noncombustible material protects the floor from heat and sparks.

Ash pit
Ashes are dumped through an opening in the hearth into the fireproof storage compartment below. Many fireplaces today omit the ash pit.

Foundation
Usually a reinforced concrete slab; holds concentrated weight of masonry fireplace and chimney structures.

masonry and prefabricated rather than by mode of heating.

The choice is not as absolute as it may sound. The wide range of styles available in each category allows you to have the appearance of one type and the performance of another.

Masonry fireplaces

Though masonry fireplaces are difficult and costly to build, they continue to be popular for several valid reasons. Not only are masonry fireplaces strong and durable, they lend an air of structural solidity to the house they serve. Brick or stone adds a quiet beauty both inside and out. Perhaps most important, these materials impart feelings of permanence and stability because of the long traditions behind them. (Many people find it impossible to imagine keeping the home fires burning in a free-form, freestanding metal fireplace.)

For those who wish the durability and strength but not the nostalgia, masonry fireplaces can be fitted to modern decor by a facing of tile, decorative concrete, mirrored glass, or polished metal. Though the long wall is the traditional location for a living room fireplace, you're likely to find a modern design tucked away in a corner, acting as a room divider, or freestanding.

Because of their great weight—most are about 5,000 pounds—masonry fireplaces usually are found on the ground floor, though they can be stacked one above the other in two-story buildings. Because of their considerable bulk, most are built on outside walls if they come as an addition to an existing building. In new construction they may be located on inside or outside walls with equal ease, assuming there is no difference in grade levels.

Satisfactory fires depend upon some close relationships: firebox opening to firebox volume to damper size to chimney size and height. The basic arithmetic is fairly well worked out, but other fine shadings of shape and proportion require a skilled designer and careful masonry work. These design details can be circumvented by use of a prefabricated metal insert that includes a firebox, damper, and smoke dome. Such metal inserts come in both conventional and heat-circulating types, but still the masonry work demands professional skills. (Heat-circulating types may be made especially complex by their ductwork if this extends as flexible tubing rather than being incorporated into the shell of the fireplace.)

There is a less critical form of masonry that can be executed by homeowners. Concrete blocks can be stacked and reinforced properly by a moderately skilled amateur builder. (The design factors remain critical—and can be harder to control because of the large size of concrete blocks.) Concrete blocks also are less expensive than brick.

Prefabricated metal fireplaces

These fireplaces come in each of the major types—conventional, heat-circulating, and freestanding. (The first two are called "built-ins.") They all share the same basic advantages: relatively low cost, ease of installation, and freedom of location, thanks to their light weight (600 to 800 pounds with facing).

A prefabricated built-in unit automatically takes care of the critical relationships of fireplace opening size to volume of firebox to damper size, that must be resolved in designing a masonry fireplace.

Most prefabricated units of all types have zero clearance ratings—they can be placed directly against combustible walls and floors, which can mean an appreciable saving in space.

Almost all of these units also carry approval tags of one or more of the nationally recognized inspection agencies. These agencies include the International Conference of Building Officials (ICBO), Building Officials Code Administration (BOCA), and Southern Building Code Congress (SBCC). In addition, most of these fireplaces are listed as safe appliances by Underwriters Laboratories (UL). They have acquired general acceptance in local building codes.

The metal boxes may not last as long as a masonry fireplace lined with firebrick, but their record of durability is good.

The heat-circulating fireplace

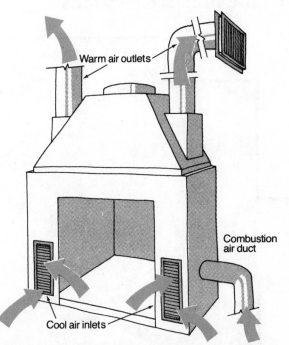

Efficient, versatile. Air warmed by a heat-circulating fireplace is returned to the same room by most units, but some —like the one shown here—can duct warmth into another room.

Both masonry and prefabricated metal fireplaces are described more completely in the chapters beginning on page 64. See especially pages 64–73 for masonry and 74–87 for prefabricated metal.

Planning fireplace location

When fireplaces were the sole source of heat for both comfort and cooking, they were found in almost every room in a substantial house. Wherever they've been relegated to a role of supplemental heat source, it is rare to find more than one or two in a home.

The single fireplace usually is located where household members congregate to relax, converse, pursue leisure activities, and entertain guests—in the main living room or the family room.

But the fireplace's historical roles still point to useful ideas for other locations. Kitchen fireplaces offer a cook such fine possibilities as Dutch ovens, barbecue grills, even hooks from which to hang simmering pots. For an intimate fireside, the suitable rooms include dens, studies, bedrooms, or even that ultimate refuge, the bathroom.

If you've been thinking about a fireplace for some time, chances are you know in some detail where you want it and how you want it to look. Even so, asking yourself a few questions about your reasons for wanting a fireplace will help pinpoint some decisions. How often will you have fires? With whom will you share them? Are they mainly romantic additions to an atmosphere, or will they be necessary sources of heat? The next section can help you both ask and answer these kinds of questions.

Fitting the fireplace to the room

At a holiday party, a generous fireplace attracts a dozen souls and more with its spreading warmth. On any wintry night, a cozy little fireside invites two, but no more, to pull their chairs up close for the peace and quiet.

Fitting a fireplace into a household means fitting it to both people and space. If the fire is to warm guests almost as often as it does the family, the hearth will need to be big enough to warm a throng, and the room big enough to hold one. At the other extreme, a hideaway fireplace will serve best if the scale is as intimate as the place.

This much is easy. But effective and functional placement calls for more than correct size and general location. For example, putting the fireplace opening too close to a door can produce drafts that billow smoke into the room, or cause unwanted traffic between the fire and those it warms. In short, you

Possible fireplace locations

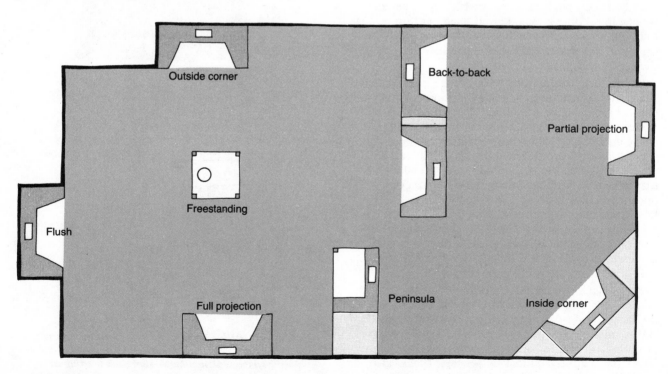

Outside corner

Back-to-back

Partial projection

Freestanding

Flush

Full projection

Peninsula

Inside corner

need to locate your fireplace not only in a satisfactory room, but in a satisfactory place within that room.

Size and shape of the room. Both of these factors are important in locating the fireplace and in determining its size. In a small room, you probably will be restricted to one or two wall locations. A large room offers more possibilities—and more pitfalls.

The most efficient fireplace for heating a large room is a freestanding type centrally placed to radiate heat in all directions. In addition to being heat-efficient, the prefabricated metal type is the simplest fireplace type to install. On the other side of the coin, a centrally placed freestanding fireplace cuts sharply into usable floor space and limits furniture placement.

If a room is square or nearly so, a fireplace can be located with equal efficiency on either a side or end wall. But, if a fireplace is located on the end wall of a long, narrow room, the fire's heat may never reach the other end. Also, guests will tend to crowd around the fireplace, leaving the opposite end empty even if you put the hors d'oeuvres there. As in the case of centrally placed freestanding fireplaces, furniture placement becomes difficult. For these reasons, in such rooms the fireplace customarily is located near the center of one long wall.

For similar reasons the corner fireplace is suited best to square or nearly square rooms.

A fireplace wall or partial wall can be used effectively to break one over-large room into a pair of more comfortable spaces either as a remodeling project or in the designing of a new house. A typical division would turn a gigantic living room into a living room and den, or living room and dining room. Such a wall can be a peninsula (as shown in the sketch on the facing page) or an island.

With a wall of this type, the opportunity exists to install two fireplaces back-to-back. (In trade talk, all such fireplaces are back-to-back because the openings face in opposite directions; in fact, the fireboxes may be back-to-back or side-by-side.) The temptation may arise to design a fireplace with two opposed openings and a single flue. This can be done, but such fireplaces tend to draw poorly unless designed by a master. It is much easier to build a chimney with two flues leading to separate fireboxes.

Irregularly shaped rooms present special problems for any fireplace that heats primarily by radiation, because infrared rays travel only in a straight line. To heat as much of the room as possible, the fireplace must be placed for optimum radiation.

One other aspect of placement has to do with the relationship of fireplace to wall. To save space, the entire depth of the fireplace and chimney can be outside the wall. To allow for a shallow set of shelves to flank a fireplace on one or both sides, the firebox and chimney can be half in, half out. To make a maximum

design effect where space is no object, the whole depth of the fireplace can be inside the wall.

Fireplace size. The size of a room does much to determine the size of a fireplace in both technical and esthetic terms. A huge firebox in a tiny room will bake the occupants before it cheers them. Conversely, a tiny firebox in a ballroom will warm neither body nor soul.

The chart below establishes some conventional relationships of fireplace opening to room size. (Builders of conventional or freestanding masonry fireplaces must take into account that all of the firebox and flue dimensions relate to the size of the opening; details of these relationships are described on page 65.)

Meanwhile, facings can vary enormously in proportion to openings, to give more or less emphasis to a fireplace as the designer sees fit. Even so, there are limits. The firebox cannot be a peephole in a mass of stone, nor can a huge firebox look plausible surrounded by a matchstick frame in an otherwise flat wall.

Good proportions

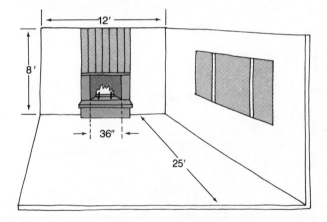

Suggested Width of Fireplace Openings appropriate to size of a room		
Size of Room In Feet	Width of Fireplace Opening in Inches	
	If in Short Wall	If in Long Wall
10 x 14	24	24 to 32
12 x 16	28 to 36	32 to 36
12 x 20	32 to 36	36 to 40
12 x 24	32 to 36	36 to 48
14 x 28	32 to 40	40 to 48
16 x 30	36 to 40	48 to 60
20 x 36	40 to 48	48 to 72

Traffic patterns. The flow of traffic through a room affects the choice of location. Traffic patterns are determined by doorways and—less rigidly—by fur-

Controlling traffic

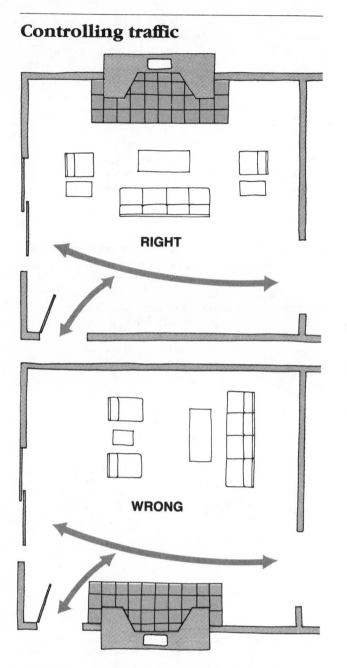

RIGHT

WRONG

niture placement. Locate the fireplace where traffic through the room will not have to pass between furniture and fireplace, and provide a path so the firetender is not forced to trample over guests while working.

A more subtle consideration is line-of-sight views of activity outside the fireside circle. Being able to see into other rooms can break the feeling of intimacy a fireplace should create.

Drafts. When you locate a fireplace opposite an outside door, gusts of wind may cause an uneven flow of air whenever the door opens. Smoke then billows into the room. To prevent such drafts, locate the fireplace as shown in the drawing of a good traffic

pattern (at left), or build a fairly solid room divider between the fireplace and the source of moving air.

Particularly sensitive to drafts are fireplaces with two or more open sides, and most sensitive of all is the freestanding fireplace with suspended metal hood. With these, even the faint air currents stirred by someone walking past may cause smoke to eddy into the room. The most effective cure is to place furniture so that people cannot walk close by the fireplace.

Structural limitations. Fireplace location may be limited by the house structure itself. In new home construction, fireplaces are easier—and less expensive—to install than those added to an existing house.

If you are adding a fireplace, consider the structural changes you must make to accommodate a hearth, the firebox itself, and a chimney. A masonry fireplace, in particular, is more easily added to an exterior wall than an interior one because the foundation and chimney can be built outside. This minimizes structural alteration and loss of floor space. Prefabricated built-in fireplaces, on the other hand, require no foundation, and many have chimneys that can be fitted between studs and joists, so these often can be placed on an inside wall without major structural changes. Freestanding units may be placed even more freely within existing buildings.

Multiple-story buildings pose special challenges to those who wish to add a fireplace. Chimney runs are longer. If inside, they rob upstairs rooms of space, require extra framing, and must avoid gas and water pipes and electrical wiring. But there's at least one advantage: if a masonry fireplace is what you want, you might look for a location that will allow you to have a hearth on the lower floor and stack one above it at a relatively small additional cost.

Multiple flues. *Never* vent more than one fireplace, stove, or other open-flame burner into a single flue. If you plan to vent other burners into the fireplace chimney, each additional source of flame will require its own flue.

A chimney may contain two, three, even four flues, a circumstance that eliminates the need to build a separate chimney for each source of flame. Multiple-flue chimneys most often are used with back-to-back fireplaces and fireplaces located one above the other in two-story houses. The chimney of a kitchen fireplace often includes a second flue to vent a gas or woodburning range, or barbecue grill. Another possibility with a kitchen fireplace is to have a barbecue grill on the outside of the unit if it can be placed on a patio or deck.

Fireplaces often are built with an extra, unused flue for future additions. It is easier and less expensive to build an additional flue into the chimney originally than to add one later to serve a wood stove or other

Stacking fireplaces

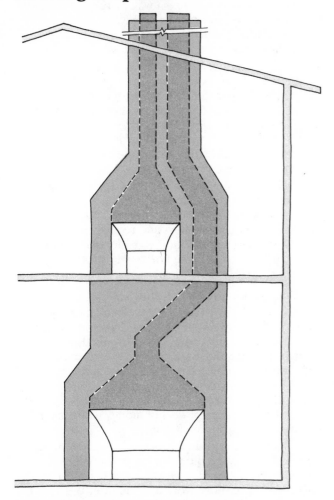

heat source. Further notes on multiple flues can be found on page 65.

Other design factors. Two other factors may weigh in the decision to locate a fireplace. One is convenient wood storage. The other is ash removal.

The need for inside wood storage will become readily apparent if ever you find yourself slogging through late night rain or snow to bring in armloads of wood. The ideal solution is a through-the-wall woodbox that can be loaded from outside, used from inside. A weathertight one minimizes heat loss from open doors. Also efficient is a bin built into the fireplace itself—alongside, or beneath a raised hearth. Ideas are shown on page 24, 33, 37, and 53.

Masonry fireplaces set on foundations may be both costly and weighty, but they do offer the boon of an ash dump beneath the firebox. Zero-clearance prefabricated fireplaces cannot do so readily. If you can include an ash dump, keep in mind that the most efficient kinds have two doors, one in the bottom of the firebox for dumping the ashes, the other at the bottom of the foundation for removing them.

The face of the fireplace

In the end, the face of the fireplace has a great deal to do with how well it satisfies its owners. This, rather than firebox dimensions or weight or heat efficiency, is where a fireplace either looks the way a fireplace should, or looks like a pale imitation of what you wanted from the start.

The range of materials offers every possibility from Lincoln log cabin to Renaissance Italian to candidate for first fireplace on a rocket ship.

The eternal rule of pleasing design is that all the components must fit together, and also must fit the rest of the room...Louis XIV does not go with Art Deco, much less with Bauhaus; a flagstone hearth looks a bit out of place with a brushed steel vertical facing. In addition, the material has to fit a traditional style...it is hard to achieve authentic Louis XIV with fieldstone, impossible with stainless steel. Even so, every style offers options. Hearth and facing can be of different materials, though one should not be rustic while the other is ultramodern.

The components

It is useful to begin thinking about the exterior design of a fireplace by defining the components: hearth, mantel, and vertical facing or hood.

Hearth. The hearth—sometimes called the front hearth or fore hearth—is the noncombustible material that protects the adjoining floor from sparks, runaway logs, and heat radiated from the fire. Almost all hearths are of a masonry material.

On any fireplace set into or against a wall, the front hearth must extend code-required distances beyond the front opening and to each side of it. A freestanding fireplace or wood stove must be placed on or suspended over a hearth of a size determined by the size of the unit and local building codes.

Most hearths are either flush with the floor or raised above it. Space often dictates the choice: small rooms need flush hearths so traffic can move; large rooms adapt well to raised hearths to help draw attention to the fireplace. Raised hearths can be solid or cantilevered. Cantilevered types can provide underneath storage. Both provide platforms for container plants or other decorations, and, if high enough, extra seating. Rarely, hearths are sunken to form the floor of a conversation pit.

Mantel. When the fireplace was used consistently to cook the family meals, the mantel was one of its working parts, a storage shelf for pots and pans, condiments, and bowls or dishes full of food that needed to be kept warm. As cookstoves replaced fireplaces in the kitchen, the mantel lost its function. Freed, it became one of the easiest ways to key the fireplace to the architectural or decorative style of a room.

In most informal designs the mantel is a horizontal shelf, no more. Several traditional formal designs match the horizontal shelf with a vertical piece at each side of the fireplace opening.

Some mantels are shelves formed as part of a masonry or metal facing, but a majority are of wood shaped or finished to fit a style. They can be ordered custom-made from mills or carvers. Manufacturers also supply them as prefabricated pieces made from wood or molded from synthetic materials.

Some modern fireplace designs do away with mantels altogether.

Hoods. These come in two forms, wall-mounted and suspended or supported over a freestanding fireplace. Because of weight considerations, most are metal, but they can be of masonry in a metal frame, or plaster over a metal frame.

One disadvantage of hoods is that they do not draw smoke efficiently until well warmed. Because metal heats quickly, the disadvantage is less with metal hoods than with masonry ones. (The slow draw has meant that many wall-mounted hoods are merely decorative disguises set above typical assemblies of firebox, smoke dome, and flue.)

Facing. The vertical surface around a fireplace opening is the facing. It can be of any size up to and including the whole wall that contains the fireplace. Any material that will make a wall can be used as vertical facing.

Materials for facing

In most cases, most of the exterior parts of a fireplace are of a masonry material. However, as the definitions of these parts have shown, metal and wood also come into play. This section introduces the widely used materials with some comment on possible styles for each. There also are some practical considerations. Finally, cross-referencing makes this section a partial index to examples of differing materials shown in the color photographs, pages 17–63.

Before describing the individual choices, it should be noted that most of the masonry materials weigh heavily. A facing made with them may not require extra support if it attaches to a bearing wall, but may require extra bracing or even a whole new underpinning if the fireplace fits into a nonbearing wall, or is over a weak spot. The problem is most likely to arise with prefabricated metal fireplaces since they are lightweight enough to be located anywhere in a house.

Brick. Fire and brick are peculiarly suited to each other. The warm tones of clay brick blend amiably with the orange of the flames and the ruby glow of the coals. Even when no fire is burning, the mellow bricks seem to suggest the promise of fire.

Bricks do not have to be laid in conventional courses. They may be laid up-ended or stacked to produce a strong vertical line; they may be laid in massive numbers to make a wall or partition; or, to break up space, they may even be set into the wall in the familiar patterns of the garden walk— herringbone, crisscross, or basket weave.

The two types of bricks most generally used for facing are known as common brick and face brick. Common is a porous, rough type, usually used for inner surfaces that do not show. Face brick is a hard-surfaced type, usually used for fireplace facings. If you plan to paint over the brickwork, use common bricks. Clay bricks come in a range of colors, from red through coral to buff.

Used bricks suggest another possibility. These bricks, with bits of mortar adhering to them, make a pleasant facing for informal interiors. You can look for them at housewreckers and regular masonry suppliers. Another variation is the long, thin Roman brick, which gives strong horizontal lines.

Stone. As a building material, stone comes in many shapes, sizes, colors, and textures.

Weathered stone offers a range of all these qualities. River rock is somewhat polished and rounded; fieldstone—weathered only by air—tends to be rough textured and angular. Both can, of course, be of almost any geologic type. They are at their most effective in rustic decors, especially in their native sites. The property owner who can find stone for the taking can save a great deal of money while gaining a uniquely appropriate fireplace.

Cut stone can be almost as rugged as weathered stone if only rough-quarried (as sandstone often is), or it can be polished to elegance (as marble and slate often are). The more work and the rarer the type, the more expensive stone becomes. Examples of stone work are shown on pages 56–57.

Ceramic tile. Because its colors, patterns, and textures vary from rough to glazed, earth tones to iridescent, solid color to handpainted designs, ceramic tile can contribute to formal Old World decors or contemporary ones. Though tile is most popular as a hearth material, it also can be used as a decorative border around a fireplace opening or applied in mass to the surrounding wall.

It is intermediate in weight and can be applied over many existing wall surfaces. (See the *Sunset* book *Remodeling with Tile* for detailed instructions in application techniques.) Prices vary as much as appearance, but even the lower range is relatively expensive compared to other materials. For examples of tile with fireplaces, see pages 17, 18–21, 24, 30, and 33.

Concrete. As a facing or hearth, it is available as precast panels, or formed. While still plastic it can be tooled, troweled, brushed, floated, or polished to provide different textures. It also can be sculpted.

Onyx or marble chips can be set into it, then ground smooth and polished to make terrazzo. If these options are not enough, it can be stained or painted to allow a range of colors.

When pouring concrete holds no attraction, the material can be bought as plain or decorative blocks and stacked up, like bricks or adobe.

In short, concrete is enormously versatile as well as relatively inexpensive among the masonry materials.

Examples of concrete hearths are to be found on the front cover as well as on pages 27 and 46. Concrete-faced fireplaces are shown on pages 27 and 52.

Adobe. Spanish Colonial styles dominate where adobe is used as a hearth and facing material. Though it comes in blocks, adobe often is used in curved forms. Not infrequently, the blocks are plastered over and painted, but tradition also allows them to be left exposed and unpainted.

They tend to be heavier than brick or concrete blocks, but less heavy than stone. Adobe blocks may not be readily available outside the Southwest. For examples, see pages 39 and 62.

Synthetic masonry. If a conventional masonry wall appears impractical for weight or other reasons, several lightweight synthetic materials may be substituted. These range from thin veneers that look like brick to expanded volcanic rock weighing less than a quarter as much as natural stone of similar size. Building supply stores can help you survey the possibilities.

Wood. Mostly, one thinks of wood as useful for feeding the fire. However, wood goes around the fireplace opening to good effect. Most often it is used for the mantel, but it also can be used as a facing.

Through milling or carving, mantels may be custom-made to fit any decor. Some notable examples of wood mantels are to be found on pages 24, 30–31, 33, and 41.

As facings, carved wood panels belong with many elegant periods of European interior design, notably including those of Renaissance Italy and the France of the Kings Louis XIV and XV. Plainer wood panels have been a part of modern American design. As rough-sawn boards—pecky cedar or barn siding—wood facings also fit into rustic decors.

Costs of wood range widely, depending on both variety and the complexity of carving or milling. Otherwise, wood has only two modest practical limitations: it may require more maintenance than other materials, and it must be installed so that no wood edges are in direct line with flames. The basic code requirement is that wood be set back at least 6 inches on either side, and 12 inches across the top of the firebox opening. Successful fireplaces with wood facings are shown on pages 22, 30, 31, and 52.

Metals. Copper, brass, bronze, iron, and steel all have been used as facings for fireplaces. Most commonly, metal is used as a hood, but it also can serve as regular vertical facing.

The softer metals—copper and brass—may be used in smooth sheets, or may be formed, embossed, or otherwise given textured or patterned surfaces. Sheet steel can be brushed, polished, or—for color—anodized. Iron usually comes in the form of wrought ornaments to complement andirons and tools rather than as a surfacing material.

Advantages of metal include durability, light weight (especially valuable for hoods suspended over free-standing masonry fireplaces), and adaptability to the designs of many eras. Typically, metals are expensive compared to the other common materials.

Examples of successful installations using metal facings are on pages 21, 26, and 29.

Where to get help

You may find you need professional help in design or installation, or both.

Design help may come from an architect, a specialist contractor, the dealer from whom you buy your fireplace, or some combination of these. An architect may be hired to do the design only, or to design the work and let the contracts. Specialized contractors—often listed under "Fireplaces" in the Yellow Pages—have repertories of stock designs which they offer as part of their contract obligation to install. Dealers in fireplaces or fireplace materials also may have stock designs, but less ability than a contractor to work with you in your home on details.

For any dealings, get referrals. Reputable individuals or companies are willing to provide references or referrals to completed jobs. In addition to checking with former customers, it is prudent to inquire at nonprofit consumer protection agencies.

If you hire a contractor to do the installation, check first with the state Contractor Licensing Board, which will tell you if the firm is licensed, bonded, and insured for worker's compensation.

Once you choose a firm, every agreement between you and the contractor should appear in a final, written contract. A good contract will include 1) a completion date; 2) a complete listing of materials and services (including brand names and model numbers of all fireplace and chimney components the contractor is to purchase); 3) all manufacturer and contractor guarantees and warranties; 4) a payment schedule, ideally arranged in three installments (down payment, completion payment, and final payment at the end of any lien period); and 5) agreement on who will provide service in case of malfunction.

A GALLERY OF IDEAS

In this gallery you'll find an array of adaptable designs for fireplaces, hearths, and mantels, and even ideas for fireside room settings. There are boldly assertive designs, as well as fireplaces that practically melt into the wall—all in a variety of styles ranging from the dramatically original to the elegantly traditional. Many are simple enough to add to an existing house; others are so stellar as to have an entire house planned around them. But beauty is more than skin deep; more and more, a fireplace is expected to contribute to the total home heating effort, and the following pages include many that do. Fireplaces that incorporate heat-saving features are indicated by this special symbol: ϵ HEAT EFFICIENT

The crackling blaze on the family hearth has a truly universal, even atavistic, appeal. As long as there have been houses, people have felt the tug of this appeal, and the design of the fireplace has received special attention.

Today's fireplaces come in sizes ranging from tiny to truly baronial. Though traditionally located in the living area, they are now found in virtually any room of the house, even the bathroom. Materials vary, too—brick, stone, metal, glass, wood ... almost any material is fair game for the contemporary designer.

The energy question. Along with attention to visual design has come increasing attention to function. The fireplace can be a better heater than before. In some cases, circulating fireplaces can take over a substantial part of the duties of a central heating system. Freestanding metal units also offer a heating bonus, since their metal parts, when heated, provide extensive radiant surface area. And conventional fireplaces can be fitted with various heat-reclaiming devices or located in such a way that their performance as heaters is optimal, if less than the other two types.

Look for this symbol: ϵ HEAT EFFICIENT. It indicates a fireplace that has an energy-saving feature or design. We've placed the symbol on all circulating fireplaces, metal freestanding units, wood stoves, and fireplaces located to radiate maximum heat or fitted with heat-saving accessories. And remember that many of the designs not bearing the energy-bonus symbol can be made more efficient either by substituting a circulating unit for a conventional one or by adding one or more heat-reclaiming devices.

If wood is to be your primary heat source, you may want to look at wood stoves. Their efficiency is unmatched, and in some cases a stove can be fitted to an existing fireplace. You'll find representative stoves and "retrofits" on pages 58-61. For more information see the *Sunset* book *Homeowner's Guide to Wood Stoves.*

Keeping the home fires burning. It's now easier than ever. Modern techniques allow you to create almost any shape you desire, and prefabricated conventional and circulating units make construction direct and simple. Freestanding metal fireplaces and wood stoves are the most adaptable of all—they practically "drop in."

You'll find all of these in our gallery. Though the energy-bonus symbol denotes those offering an extra measure of heat saving, all the fireplaces portrayed here have a timeless warmth, charm, and grace.

Happy meeting of form & function
"Two-story" brick fireplace frames fire and next several loads of fuel. Traditionally styled, fireplace and hearth blend effectively with decor and provide a setting for owners' collection of antique Delft tiles. Architect: Alfred T. Gilman. Design: Windom Hawkins.

Fireplaces that take center stage

Simple hearth for a multipurpose wall
Prefabricated metal firebox with simple tile facing effectively divides storage wall of bookshelves, cabinets, art display, and built-in stereo speakers. Simple materials—gypsum board and redwood—yield an elegant result. Architect: Peter Behn.

Drama in glass, tile, concrete
Massive and serene, this fireplace harmonizes display, seating, and a warm blaze. Structural wall of slumpblock wraps fireplace, penetrating the glass, while ample firebox allows wood storage to one side. Indirect sun lights the glass-walled display niche at left. Architects: Buff and Hensman.

Going up: Giving scale to a lofty space
Decorative cloth hanging is changed seasonally on this high, dramatic hearth facing.
Structural wall with integral two-way firebox is angled toward the view; behind is a cozy
conversation pit for a more intimate enjoyment of the fire. Architect: Ron Yeo.

...more attention getters

Bold design, traditional feeling
Chimney facing marches straight up the wall and back overhead, has the look of traditional carved paneling. Graceful arch is complemented by stained-glass portholes, each slightly different from the other. Storage units on either side are also near-matches, yet different: TV hides at left; extra seating is provided at right. Architect: Robert Peterson. Stained glass: Peter Mollica.

Formal order, modern feeling
Flanked by display niches, quietly dramatic fireplace takes center stage. Wall with its enclosing wings divides living area from master bedroom behind. Construction is simple—it's a prefabricated firebox—yet distinguished by subtle touches, such as allowing the chimney facing to "float" between the display niches and the ceiling. The owners occasionally use it to show slides. The hearth doubles as extra seating for parties. Architects: Buff and Hensman.

Lost space regained

What to do with that awkward under-stairs space is a problem neatly solved here. The lines of the fireplace are carried over into the lines of the staircase, with a complementary arch added at right. The resulting design brings the fireplace into the room, creating space for storage at either side. Architects: Richard Ellmore Associates.

Metal makes the difference

Copper chimney facing and mantel bring drama to a basic fireplace of painted brick. Sheets are joined with standing seams for more design interest. Hearth becomes built-in seat, its quarry tile complementing both copper and flame. Design: W. R. Queirolo.

Fireplaces & walls: Some imaginative match-ups

Elegant simplicity
Steel-bordered opening punctuating the diagonal paneling gives a subtly dramatic effect.
Simple hearth is a marble slab. Design: Q-Rolo Sheet Metal Products.

Clean, functional design
Wall around prefabricated firebox contains wealth of
storage space behind hardwood-veneer cabinet doors.
Architects: Buff and Hensman

Wall of niches
Rustic wall incorporates niches for art display, with a sim-
ple cutout for the fireplace. Architect: William Churchill.
Wall and interior design: Sherman Nobleman.

Wall of glass & fire
The bold geometry of this nearly-all-glass wall is barely disturbed by the insertion of a prefabricated metal fireplace. Black tile and red-painted flue create color accents while offering a minimum silhouette for warmth from the sun. Architects: Batter/Kay. Interior design: John Snyder.

...imaginative match-ups

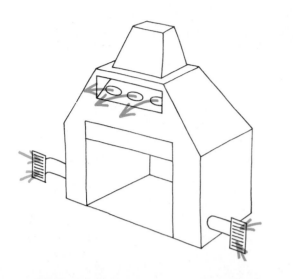

Drawing shows built-in metal firebox used in fireplace below. Vents at either side draw in cool air; the air is heated between the double walls of the fireplace, then released through tubes above the firebox.

Matching the decor

Prefabricated fireplace and wood-storage unit blend well with the clean, modern lines of this living room. The simple raised hearth maintains the room's light, airy feeling. Oak trim and dark glazed tile repeat the colors of the furnishings, helping to unify the design. Architects: Morgan and Lindstrom.

Geared for efficiency

The owners of this house get a lot out of the subtly curving wall shown here. The heat-circulating fireplace is equipped with glass doors for maximum draft control, and the flue is left exposed to increase the radiant surface area of the unit and heat the upper level through the opening above. Intake and exhaust grilles are set off by plain white marble, complemented by a black marble hearth, cut to follow the curve of the wall. Built-in cabinets and stereo speakers carry the line into the rest of the room. Architect: James L. Cutler.

Harmony in concrete

Forming hearth, fireplace, and structural wall as a seamless unit, the architect was able to harmonize fireplace and house. Complementary niches—one deep, one shallow—break the plane of the wall, lending visual interest. The exposed aggregate and wood accents help to lighten the effect. Architect: James W. P. Olson. Interior design: Jean Jongeward.

Hearth & floor are one

The handsome Mexican tile floor is here used to form the hearth, and is actually carried part-way into the firebox itself. A decorative band of glazed Mexican tile sets off both fireplace and wood storage. The openings break the symmetry of the room but not the harmony of the design. Design: John L. Sevison.

Plaster plus prefab equals Mediterranean

At left, a prefabricated metal firebox and its attendant stud framing combine with gypsum board and plaster to create a distinctly Mediterranean effect. The play of light and shadow, together with a single bright tapestry, creates the only decoration. Architect: Richard Ellmore Associates.

Distinctive designs with metal, concrete, mirrors

A radical departure

Dramatic concrete cylinder forms the fireplace and chimney in this adventurous design. Visionary architecture of the home called for a real departure in the fireplace design, and concrete was a logical choice of material. Fireplace and integral wing wall were cast in place; marks of the wooden forms match the ceiling, are the only decoration. Architect: John Lautner. Fireplace designer and project architect: Warren Lawson.

Functional futurism (left) ∈ HEAT EFFICIENT

Bold design of the home at left is fully matched by its fireplace. Heavy-wall tubing begins as a log grate at the bottom, travels up the back wall, crossing through the flue in the manner of a circulating fireplace. Basically an extra-large convection grate, the design boosts heating by drawing cool air in at the bottom, heating it, then discharging it at the top through the handsome stainless-steel hood. Architect: Wendell Lovett.

In the master's steps

Frank Lloyd Wright pioneered this technique that combines the look of stonework with the versatility of poured concrete. After wooden forms are erected, concrete is poured in around stones placed as the work proceeds. The result can be dramatic, as shown here. Design: Mark Mills.

It's all mirror
Fire burns in a reflection of the room; every face of hearth, mantel, and fireplace surround is a mirror. Trompe l'oeil effect adds a dash of the unexpected to the simple decor. Interior design: Mary Beth Stone.

Mirror, mirror, on the wall
Brass and white marble mark the fireplace in this mirror-wall. The large mirrors—there are two—greatly expand the feeling of space, giving extra scale to the master bedroom suite. Interior design: Anne Lear.

...distinctive designs

Light creates a painting
Like an ever-changing abstract painting, a single sheet of stainless steel reflects the passage of the day; at night, it has its own light. Copper sheeting, chemically treated for an antique look, frames the steel and the prefabricated metal firebox. Design: John Reis and Q-Rolo Sheet Metal Products.

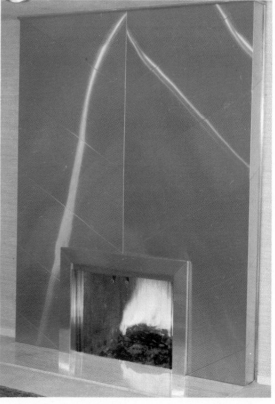

Finely finished
Cleanly executed design in brass and stainless steel sets off a masonry firebox and marble hearth. Subtle play of reflections changes with the position of the viewer. Design: Margo Deane and Q-Rolo Sheet Metal Products.

Traditional mantels: Timeless & graceful

Making the new look old

Much of what appears to be old wood stripped of its paint is actually new, painstakingly crafted to blend with the wainscoting of a classic home; the only original piece is the mantel itself. The vine pattern in the tile was handpainted to match the rug, and all the new woodwork was given a wash coat of white gesso to make it match the paneling in both color and texture. Fabric over the mantel provides a finishing touch. Design: Stacey-Steele, Russell Lowrey.

Paneled beauty

Stand-out mantelpiece matches the fine paneling of this stately home. Integrating the fireplace in this way helps to keep it from overly dominating the room, yet permits use of a large firebox and hearth—in this case, they are marble. Architects: Arthur B. Clark & Birge M. Clark.

A retrofit

Scouting the antique auctions paid off for the owners of this handsome old mantelpiece; it's a perfect fit for their contemporary home. Brass fireplace surround helps it harmonize. The built-in shelves—and even the firebox in summer—are home to the family's house plants. Architect: Everett Tozier.

Mini mock-Tudor

The shape of early English fireplaces is echoed in this older home. Open-beamed ceiling is an ancestor of the modern one above left, the shape of the fireplace emphasizing the room's vertical dimensions. Molded plaster relief borders the fire.

Simple & straightforward

A good basic design in painted wood and brick can go with almost any decor. Here, its understated elegance is set against the clean lines of contemporary furnishings.

Family hearths: More than a place for the fire

Roomy, multipurpose hearth

Generous extended hearth offers plenty of room for wood storage, extra seating. Precast concrete beam is both lintel and mantel, supporting the brickwork above it and echoing the shape and size of the roof beams. In a house of sports fans, the TV niche—it's behind the door to left of clock—is a welcome addition for an afternoon of football before the fire. Architect: Ron Yeo.

Tying the room together

Multipurpose storage wall seems to "notch in" to fireplace surround, which in turn ties it to soffit at right. Hearth extends the full distance from one flanking wall to the other. Distinctive relief and tile work were designed and executed by the owners. Architect: Michael Moyer.

Hearth & side table are one

A raised hearth that becomes a side table was created by the step-down floor of this family room. Hearth extends the full width of the area, providing space for board games, TV, lamp, and bookshelves. Architect: Vern K. Cooley/TRA.

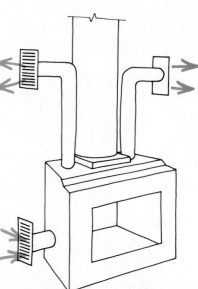

Rustic & efficient ⊖ HEAT EFFICIENT

Natural stone and clear heart redwood milled from trees felled on the property distinguish the fireplace of this cabin in the woods. But the beauty is more than skin-deep; most of the cabin's heat comes from the fireplace, a prefabricated, fan-driven, circulating unit (see drawing, above). Ample hearth provides seating and space for firewood brought into the house through doors to either side of fireplace. There's a large woodbox behind the doors that can be loaded from the outside.

A hearth for all seasons
Sunny window seat is actually an extension of the raised hearth running around two sides of the living room. Tile-accented antique mantel seems right at home in its new setting.
Architect: George Suyama.

A cozy den
Stained glass and brick lend a note of intimacy to this warm, inviting den. Herringbone pattern of the chimney facing adds variety to the brickwork, is consistent with the traditional feeling. Design: Bob Dutton.

Scale it down
Traditional mantel and chimney facing retain the old-world feeling of the other fireplaces in this large house, but on a reduced scale. Architects: Arthur B. Clark & Birge M. Clark.

Accent on intimacy

Tall & narrow

Clean lines and some space-efficiency tricks help this vacation home fireplace fit right in: Hearth for the prefabricated metal firebox is an extension of the concrete entry-level floor. Angle of the fireplace saves space for the entry while the simple, brightly painted gypsum board facing complements the room's vertical proportions. Architect: Robert C. Peterson.

In a nook of its own

Located to one side of the living room, this fireplace nook is a kind of cul-de-sac in the traffic pattern of the house. Construction was simple and direct: a prefabricated firebox, gypsum board, tile, and natural wood. Space for books and firewood is at right. Architect: Peter Behn.

Conversation pits & firerooms invite a gathering

Rug-wrapped room   ℰ HEAT EFFICIENT

You always sit on the carpet in this conversation pit. Wall-to-wall carpet runs from living area down steps, finally wrapping the built-in seats themselves—a simple and economical way to create furniture. Freestanding metal fireplace radiates more heat than a built-in masonry fireplace would have. Architects: Abel and Wilkes.

Drop-in hideaway
Prefabricated metal firebox is the focal point
of this brick-walled hideaway. The pass-through
to the kitchen offers convenience and
gives you a glimpse of the stairs.
Architect: Marshall Lewis.

Extending the idea ⊖ HEAT EFFICIENT

Here, the conversation-pit idea is extended to form a room. The built-in seating can accommodate a large number of guests, yet the feeling of intimacy is not lost. Special window treatment steals some space from the patio, creating a larger hearth, while the freestanding metal fireplace offers extra radiant heat. Architect: Ron Yeo.

The fireplace room

A special room for the fire was created here, using a prefabricated metal firebox. The handsome hearth and facing are made of rusted railroad tie plates, bolted together. The design incorporates ample wood storage and a skylight—to dispel darkness in the low-ceilinged room and accent the tie plates. Architect: Bob Overstreet.

Structural drama

Something of a cross between a conversation pit and a fireroom is this design. Located in a cantilevered section of the living area, it features built-in carpeted seating for space efficiency and a small gas fireplace, glass-walled for minimum interruption of the panoramic view. Architects: Abel and Wilkes.

Two-way fireplaces: You can see beyond the flames

Recycling an old street
Cobblestones reclaimed from an old city street make up this massive fireplace-divider separating living and dining areas. Their rustic feeling harmonizes well with the used wood of the house. Design: Agnes Bourne.

Bringing the outdoors indoors
This adaptation of the see-through idea includes a view of the garden via a large sheet of tempered glass. Hearth and chimney construction is of adobe. Design: Cliff May.

Warming bed & bath
Cheerful glow of a two-way fireplace warms both the bath and bedroom of this added-on master bedroom suite. Use of a prefabricated metal fireplace helped speed construction. Design: Kimio Kimura.

To make a corner cozy

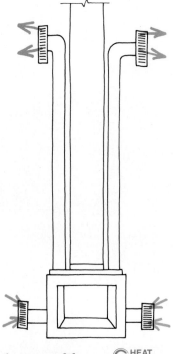

Customizing a prefab

HEAT EFFICIENT

Distinctive treatment of a prefabricated circulating fireplace is here achieved through the use of custom touches. The firescreen was made from a single sheet of glass, cut, tempered, then drilled to receive simple tubular brass handles and legs. The combustion air intake is built into the hearth, just in front of the firebox opening. Gypsum board and stud framing complete the composition. Diagram shows how air circulates through the unit. Architect: James Caldwell.

They kept their view

A little ingenuity sometimes can go a long way. Omitting the corners from two plate-glass windows left just enough room for a small prefabricated fireplace in this highly original installation. The result has minimum impact upon the view. The flue exits at an angle through the wall, while four kinds of tile harmonize to form the bi-level hearth and firebox facing. There's even room left for a small wood-storage box.

Cozy bedroom nook

Tile-faced masonry fireplace is the focal point of this inviting step-down nook, part of a master bedroom suite. Twin window seats embrace the hearth, creating plenty of room for relaxation. Architects: Moyer Associates.

Beauty with a bonus ⊖ HEAT EFFICIENT

This richly finished fireplace, set into an oblique corner, works two ways: its wide, shallow firebox reflects a maximum of heat, and the warmth of the firebrick helps heat an adjoining room. Just behind the fireplace is a massive concrete wall (Trombe wall) that is part of the home's passive solar heating system. During the day, the sun warms the wall; at night, the fireplace takes over. Architect: Daniel Lieberman.

Corners have outsides, too

Stone and concrete fireplace elegantly turns the corner at the intersection of two rooms in this graceful, traditional house. The idea is a good one and still adaptable today. Architects: Arthur B. Clark & Birge M. Clark.

Metal hoods: Decorative & functional

Copper corner

Copper sheets joined with standing seams make up this attractive fireplace hood. Steel-lined but uninsulated, the warm metal effectively improves the fireplace's heating efficiency. Part of the copper was oxidized for a variation in color. Also noteworthy is the fireplace's angle to the wall; it creates room for an outside door off the dining room. Architect: Marshall Lewis.

Room for two

The adaptability of the metal hood is well illustrated here. This one is big enough to include a wood stove and its separate flue, while visual beauty is provided by the open fire on its raised hearth. Hood is of etched steel, custom-fitted. Architect: Paul Hayden Kirk.

Sheer beauty
Pride of craftsmanship and love of beautiful materials
are embodied in this elegant design. Copper and stone
were combined with an expert hand, yielding a truly
eye-catching result. Architects: Terry & Egan.

A traditional look
Prefabricated metal hood makes for easy installation,
goes well in a variety of settings.

Freestanding metal fireplaces: Variety & an energy bonus, too

Simplicity of form & function
HEAT EFFICIENT

A three-point ceiling anchorage, a hole for the flue pipe, and it's in. In addition to ease of installation, this hanging fireplace offers a 360° view of the fire. Its design makes it extremely adaptable to a wide variety of situations, and its open firebox and warm metal surfaces radiate much of the fire's heat. Architect: James A. Jennings.

A modern classic
HEAT EFFICIENT

Views from the corner of this house were preserved through the use of a classic freestander. Its small silhouette, minimum "footprint," and metal flue help it to take up as little space as possible. Like most free-standing metal units, this one is a better heater than a conventional fireplace. Architect: James A. Jennings.

The custom approach
HEAT EFFICIENT

Dramatic custom fireplace of blue-enameled steel, with its distinctive offset chimney, is the focal point of this house's living area. Its location just off the circulation areas of the house allows it to be seen from many angles, while the small conversation pit provides a more intimate space for relaxation by the fire. Brass-bound glass doors improve control of the fire, limiting the amount of warm room air wasted up the chimney. Architects: Larsen, Lagerquist and Morris.

Ringing changes on an old idea

The form of a freestanding metal fireplace is limited only by the skills of designer and artisan. This custom fireplace is not only stylish, it's a worker. The flue extends past a second-floor balcony, helping to heat the upstairs, while the warm firebox surfaces radiate heat to the living-dining areas. The simple precast hearth is of exposed-aggregate concrete. Architect: Wendell Lovett.

...freestanding metal fireplaces

Graceful curves E HEAT EFFICIENT

A less geometric appearance is presented by this fireplace, with its curving lines and copper-plated heat shield. The top and bottom contain masses of concrete that hold the heat for later release. Architect: Leonard E. Lincoln.

An old standby E HEAT EFFICIENT

The Franklin fireplace, or stove, is an early example of the idea of getting more heat from wood. Its metal surfaces make good heat radiators, and its doors control the flow of air up the chimney. Modern ones are made just like the old ones.

The basic box E HEAT EFFICIENT

Simple metal box sits in a special niche in this handsome modern living room. In function, this fireplace is like its cousins; it differs only in shape. Architect: Jeffrey T. Garner.

These fireplaces define rooms

Organizing the room around the fire

Both the designs shown above use metal-hooded fireplaces as organizing elements for living rooms. At left, a custom-made, brass-bound steel hood is suspended over an attractively tiled masonry firepit. The fireplace divides the stairs that lead to a step-down living area and can be seen from all points in the room. Architect: Samuel Romerstein. At right, a similar fireplace, using a prefabricated conical hood, is the focal point of an octagonal living area. All interior views center on the fire. The masonry hearth has a slate-covered surface for extra seating. Architect: Don Jacobs.

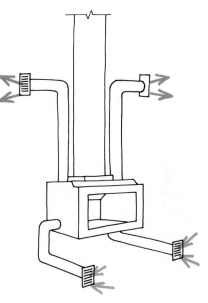

A column of stone ⊖ HEAT EFFICIENT

Massive stone column hides a circulating fireplace (see drawing for the secret of its air vents). In addition to helping support the roof, the fireplace divides entry and living areas, becoming, in effect, an interior wall. Architect: Don Jacobs.

Helping to guide traffic ⊖ HEAT EFFICIENT

Fireplace-woodbox combination acts as a freestanding divider in the large, open-planned living space of this home. Traffic tends to stay behind it, and the side shown, with its cheerful blaze, helps to create a feeling of intimacy. The handcarved plaque lends added visual interest, and the exposed fluepipe radiates extra heat into the room. Architect: Don Jacobs.

These fireplaces divide rooms

Where rooms meet

This fireplace marks the junction of four distinct living areas: at left, the entry; above right, the master bedroom; below right, the dining room; the camera is in the living room. Use of a two-sided prefabricated fireplace permits a cheering view of the fire as you enter. Architects: Abel and Wilkes.

Central heating  HEAT EFFICIENT

Extra-large circulating fireplace divides dining and living areas, its top serving as a dining room buffet counter. Prefabricated firebox was bricked in, then faced with gypsum board. Design also incorporates wood storage and cabinets. The raised hearth conceals the air inlets; exhaust vent is marked by simple cut-outs. Architects: Bardwell, Case, and Gilbert.

Brick is the buffer

Placed between living and dining areas, this large fireplace divides the open plan without restricting movement between rooms. See-through design allows fire viewing from both sides; exposed flue pipe radiates extra heat. Architect: Bill Abbott.

A sculptural divider

White-painted brick fireplace with incorporated wood storage and art display divides living and dining areas. Sculptural form is accented by a curving shelf set into the fireplace face; the shelf projects slightly on the back side. Architects: Batter/Kay.

Brick: Traditional, rustic, elegant

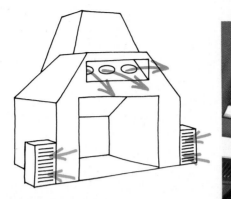

Planning pays off

Since this fireplace had to provide much of the home's heat, a circulating unit was chosen. Brick and cast concrete conceal the intake and exhaust (see diagram), making for a handsome design. Placing the cold-air duct of the home's furnace high on the wall at the right allows its fan to tap the "lake" of warm air at ceiling height, sending it on to the rest of the house. Architect: A. J. Westberg, Jr.

For a rustic effect

Used brick and used wood go hand in hand in this family room. The brick is really a structural wall doubling as a covering for a prefabricated metal firebox. The raised hearth, created by three turns in the wall, makes a cozy seat; a TV hides behind the door at right. The mantel is corbeled—each brick projects slightly beyond the one below. Architect: Ron Yeo.

Vigorous, efficient design

Brick complements the robust architecture of this all-wood house, and conceals a prefabricated circulating fireplace. The exhaust air grill was formed by simply omitting the mortar joints from the center bricks above the arch; the intakes are at the sides—you can just see one behind the post. Part of the hearth base is cantilevered, leaving space for wood storage. The freestanding design allowed for a small library behind the fireplace, and is more efficient, too, since none of the heat is conducted through an outside wall. Architect: Garrett Larsen.

The basic building block

Brick's versatility as a building material makes it a good
choice for fireplaces. Here, the simple form of the brick
is echoed in the raised hearth—which becomes a fireside
seat—and in the fireplace facing. Another thing—if its
ruddy color fights the furnishings, as it might have here,
a change is only as far away as the nearest can of paint.
Interior design: Sherman Nobleman.

Keeping the family warm

 HEAT EFFICIENT

The owners of this added family room wanted a fireplace
design that would match the traditional feeling of their
home, but they wanted real heat from it, too. Brick solved
their first problem, a prefabricated circulating fireplace the
second. The result, in used brick, is classic. The raised
hearth helps protect children, and the antique metal grill
over the exhaust air vent strikes a graceful note. Architect:
Bob Stoecker.

...brick fireplaces

Imagination at play

Brickwork can provide fertile ground for creativity to grow, as this imaginative fireplace shows. Its stepped-back top reduces the size of what might otherwise have been an overpowering fireplace and becomes an important element in the powerful, graceful design. Architects: Champion & Turner.

Plain geometry

Rectangular shapes and openings are easily achieved with bricks. This large fireplace, with its flanking wood-storage spaces, fits nicely into the overall geometric scheme of its living room. A band of wood at the top helps tie all the elements together. Architect: George Cody.

Understated elegance

"Subtle as a brick," that old sarcastic remark, loses its meaning here. In this sleek, modern design, the brick wall facing runs the width of the room, becoming the fireplace back midway. The fireplace canopy is also brick, faced with light-stained wood set off by a simple metal band. Architects: Buff & Hensman.

Not as easy as it looks

The timelessness of fine craftsmanship is well portrayed in this deceptively simple stone fireplace. Rocks were hand-selected on a local beach, then carefully laid to achieve a balance of sizes, colors, and proportions. A handsome wood mantel, joined with splines, caps it all off. Architect: James L. Cutler.

The wall is the fireplace

Stone can be used structurally, too. Here, as at right, the fireplace helps support the roof. This is ashlar—cut or hewn—stone. It's more expensive, but the look is distinctive, and it's extremely strong. Architects: Goodwin Steinberg Associates.

Stone: Rugged & earthy

Simple symmetry

Stones of relatively uniform size help to keep fireplace the from overwhelming the small living room of this vacation house. To simplify construction, a precast concrete beam was used as a lintel. Custom-made andirons and firescreen make handsome additions. Architect: Walter Sontheimer.

Stone hides a circulator ⊖ HEAT EFFICIENT

The adaptable prefabricated circulating fireplace shows its versatility in this design. The stones make up the facing only; the unit is not solid stonework. Although the exhaust-air vents are evident, you have to look hard for the intakes; they're revealed only by the open, unmortared joints just to left and right of the firebox. Final touches include a hidden combustion air intake beneath the slate hearth and an exposed flue for extra radiant heat. Architect: James L. Cutler.

A different approach

If there is such a thing as lightweight stonework, this must be it: stone panels. Smooth river rocks were embedded to half their thickness in a bed of sand the size of each panel. Then, concrete was poured on top with wire mesh added for reinforcement. The cured panels were then placed in a wooden framework surrounding a masonry firebox and metal flue. The result: a handsome stone fireplace without the customary hard labor. Architect: R. J. Matheson.

Wood stoves:
A home heating alternative

Start with the basics ⊖ HEAT EFFICIENT
Basic Scandinavian woodstove is a powerful heater. Wood-loading door has rotating plate draft control for precise fire regulation. Porcelain-enamel surface requires little care.

As good as new ⊖ HEAT EFFICIENT
If Jules Verne had designed a wood stove it might have looked like this. Although the form of wood stoves has changed, their function hasn't; this one works as well as ever. Restoration of an antique such as this makes a rewarding project.

You load it from the top   <small>**HEAT EFFICIENT**</small>

Wood drops in from above in this modern French stove with a 19th-century look. Body is lined with firebrick to retain heat and prevent burnout of the stove's metal parts. Small "footprint" helps it fit where others won't. Architect: Thomas Amsler.

Functional beauty   <small>**HEAT EFFICIENT**</small>

Heavily embossed surface of this enamelled-iron model gives it the look of old European tile stoves while adding to the radiant surface area. Flue pipe is available in matching colors. Architects: Johnson Olney Associates.

You can see the flames   <small>**HEAT EFFICIENT**</small>

Brightly colored steel jacket over an iron firebox helps ensure child's safety from burns. Tempered glass window offers a view of the fire, tilts up for an open flame or a cozy marshmallow roast.

Converting the fireplace for a wood stove

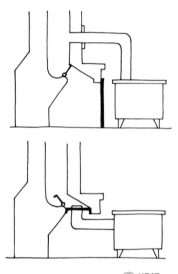

Beautiful thief reforms   ⊖ HEAT EFFICIENT

This handsome fireplace warmed diners but pulled cold air into the adjoining rooms, resulting in a net loss of heat. A small wood stove cured its bad habits. A plate in the flue adapts the stovepipe to the fireplace chimney; the drawing above shows two basic ways to do it.

It was once a barbecue   ⊖ HEAT EFFICIENT

This old outdoor barbecue is working harder now than it ever did. Its owners added a skylit family room, partly demolishing the barbecue and using its flue for a modern fireplace/stove. Stove is in constant use all season and heats much of the house. Architect: Walter Thomas Brooks.

This one was easy   ℰ HEAT EFFICIENT

If your fireplace is extra-large, sometimes a stove will fit right in, eliminating the need for a hearth extension. In this case, a switch of the damper assembly for a steel adapter plate (see drawing on facing page) was all that was needed.

Room with a view   ℰ HEAT EFFICIENT

Built into a bedroom fireplace, this thermostatically controlled cast-iron stove heats a master bedroom and bath. Open doors allow a view of the fire, close when maximum heating efficiency is desired.

Fireplaces for outdoor living

Traditional elegance
Massive traditional fireplace and mantel grace this patio, extending outdoor-living hours well into the evening. Architects: Arthur B. Clark & Birge M. Clark.

Trail's end cheer
Nothing could be more welcome after a long ride on a brisk day than this corner with its warm fire. Designed as a warming fireplace for a stable, the straightforward design—it's adobe—will be equally at home indoors when the building is someday converted into a house. Design: Cliff May.

Accessories for heat efficiency...

Turning the fireplace into a wood stove ⊖HEAT EFFICIENT

Drop-in wood stoves are available if you want to convert your fireplace. Like the one shown above, most simply slide in, sealing the opening off with a flange running around the stove. Design: Fireplace Systems, Inc.

Glass doors cut waste ⊖HEAT EFFICIENT

Add-on glass doors such as these are available to fit nearly any fireplace. They stop the waste of heated air by controlling the fire's draft. Although some radiant heat is lost, it's usually a fair trade. See page 93 for more on their use.

The tubular convection grate ⊖HEAT EFFICIENT

Log grate of c-shaped tubing draws cool air in at bottom, heats it, then emits it at the top. This natural convection improves the overall efficiency of the fireplace. A fan-powered system can be added to increase the flow of air through the grate, further boosting output. Design: Pamela Seifert.

MASONRY INSTALLATION

It is often said that a good masonry fireplace is a work of art. More to the point, it must be a work of many skills. In order for a fireplace to work properly, its builder must have considerable expertise in masonry and follow the established rules and practices of sound fireplace construction. Even the simplest brick fireplace requires many hours of painstaking work.

Because of the time and skill involved, most people elect to have a mason do the work, or at least a major portion of it. But for those who feel capable of doing the work themselves, this chapter sets forth the basic requirements of fireplace construction.

The following basic requirements have been compiled from standard craft practices and national building codes, though local codes and requirements may vary.

Foundation. Because of the considerable weight, a masonry fireplace requires a separate foundation consisting of a footing (a reinforced concrete slab) and walls built up to hearth level.

Foundation walls may be constructed of reinforced concrete, solid masonry, or hollow masonry blocks. Walls must be at least 8 inches thick. In houses built on slabs, the fireplace is often built directly on the footing.

Details for reinforcing and pouring a concrete foundation are on page 67, Step 2.

Mortar. Two separate mortar mixes are required in fireplace construction. A special refractory mortar made from fireclay mixed with water must be used in the firebox and for clay tile flue lining. Type "S" mortar (1 part Portland cement, 1/2 part hydrated lime, 4-1/2 parts mortar sand) is one of several mixes recommended for use elsewhere.

Ash pit. The ash pit should be protected from water seepage, because if the ash load becomes wet, a disagreeable ashy odor will permeate the house.

The opening in the firebox floor is covered with a hinged or pivoting cast-iron plate to allow ashes to drop into the pit below. Select a type that cannot drop accidentally into the pit when opened.

To promote easy ash removal, locate the sill of the cleanout door about 10 inches above grade and cover the bottom of the pit with mortar sloped toward the door.

For a second-story fireplace directly above a first-story one, the ash chute must be routed around the fireplace below. The slope of the chute should not be greater than 6 degrees from vertical to avoid clogging.

Facing. For safety, the nearest edge of combustible trim, paneling, or facing should be at least 8 inches from the sides of the fireplace opening and at least 12 inches above the top of the opening. But check your local building code for possible variances. Maintain a minimum clearance of 2 inches between all wood framing members and the fireplace or chimney masonry. Make the front hearth at least 8 to 12 inches wider on each side than the fireplace opening.

Firebox. Back hearth and reflecting walls should be of firebrick, 4 inches thick, bonded with fire clay mortar. Bricks are laid flat and held in place by metal ties bonded into the main masonry walls.

If you build the back wall in an upward curve sloping into the fireplace, not only rising currents of warm air but also smoke will flow into the room. To avoid a smoky fireplace, slope the back wall up in straight planes to the level of the edge of the throat. For building details, see steps 11 and 12 on page 70. Optimum firebox dimensions are given in the chart below.

Lintel. The minimum lintel required to support the masonry above the front of a moderately wide fireplace opening is an angle iron 3-1/2 by 3-1/2 by 1/4 inches, enough longer than the opening to give a 3 or 4-inch seat on the masonry. For heavy masonry and wide openings, the size and thickness of these steel lintels increase in proportion. Provision should be made for expansion by wrapping the ends with fiberglass wool or providing some means for the steel lintel to move when heated.

You can build a masonry arch successfully if, at the sides of the opening, the masonry is sufficiently reinforced to resist the thrust of the arch. The minimum thickness of the masonry arch should be at least 4 to 6 inches and preferably more to avoid possible sagging.

Damper. There are many forms of dampers, usually combined with a metal throat. Some operate with a push-and-pull handle, some with a poker, others with

Size & Shape of a Fireplace
(All measurements are in inches)

Opening width	Opening height	Firebox depth	Back wall width	Vertical back wall height	Inclined back wall height	Rectangular flue lining	Inside diameter of standard round flue lining
24	24	16 – 18	14	14	16	8-1/2 x 8-1/2	10
28	24	16 – 18	14	14	16	8-1/2 x 8-1/2	10
30	28	16 – 18	16	14	20	8-1/2 x 13	10
36	28	16 – 18	22	14	20	8-1/2 x 13	12
42	28	16 – 18	28	14	20	8-1/2 x 18	12
36	32	18 – 20	20	14	24	8-1/2 x 18	12
42	32	18 – 20	26	14	24	13 x 13	12
48	32	18 – 20	32	14	24	13 x 13	15
42	36	18 – 20	26	14	28	13 x 13	15
48	36	18 – 20	32	14	28	13 x 18	15
54	36	18 – 20	38	14	28	13 x 18	15
60	36	18 – 20	44	14	28	13 x 18	15
42	40	20 – 22	24	17	29	13 x 13	15
48	40	20 – 22	30	17	29	13 x 18	15
54	40	20 – 22	36	17	29	13 x 18	15
60	40	20 – 22	42	17	29	18 x 18	18
66	40	20 – 22	48	17	29	18 x 18	18
72	40	22 – 28	51	17	29	18 x 18	18

a twist handle. A manufactured smoke dome contains a damper with "open" and "close" chain controls that hold the damper in any desired position. You should be able to expect good results with any type that is installed according to the manufacturer's instructions. Dampers should be set loosely in place and the ends wrapped in fiberglass wool to allow for expansion.

Throat. The throat, or damper opening, should extend the full width of the fireplace opening and have an area not less than that of the flue. Up to the throat, the sides of the fireplace should be vertical; about 5 inches above the throat, the sides should start drawing into the flue. The bottom edge of the throat should be 6 to 8 inches or more above the bottom of the lintel. The throat can be formed in masonry. To save time and labor, you can install a metal prefabricated throat or smoke dome.

Smoke shelf. The smoke shelf should run the full width of the throat and be 6 to 12 inches or more front to back, depending on the depth of the fireplace. It should be given a smooth, concave surface.

Smoke dome. The smoke dome extends between the side walls from the top of the throat to the bottom of the flue. Slope the side walls at a 60° angle from the horizontal and smoothly plaster with cement mortar or an equally smooth interior surface so as not to diminish the draft action.

Flues. Flues are lined with fireclay flue tiles to protect the surrounding brickwork in the chimney from the effects of hot flue gases. Tiles should be set with fireclay mortar, and joints should be smooth to assure proper draft and to lessen creosote buildup.

Round flues are considered the most efficient for draft and smoke removal because draft-smoke columns ascend in spirals. Corners of square or rectangular flues are ineffective areas, contributing little to proper working of a flue. Square or oblong flues are frequently used, though, because they are easier to set in place.

Multiple flues. If you plan to locate two or more flues in the same chimney structure, they must be separated by at least 4 inches of a masonry material, such as brick, mortar, or concrete. This masonry divider, called a wythe, should extend 6 inches or so above the chimney top to prevent smoke from one flue from being drawn down the other. Another way to avoid this problem is to make one flue slightly taller than the other.

The size of the flue will be dictated by the size of the fireplace. The chart on page 65 gives the recommended flue sizes for sea level installations (see the paragraph "Chimney height" for information on the effect of altitude).

Flues have better draft if built as close to a vertical line as possible. When a change in direction is necessary, it should not exceed 30° from vertical nor should it reduce the flue area at the offset angle.

Chimney materials. A variety of masonry materials, including brick, concrete blocks, clay tiles, poured concrete, and stone may be used in constructing chimney walls. Following are the recommended thicknesses for walls of these materials. These thicknesses do not include the thickness of fireclay flue liner. Tall chimneys, or ones exposed to high winds, may require thicker walls—check with your building inspector.

Brick: Not less than width of standard brick (3-5/8 to 4 inches); for exterior chimney walls exposed to severe weather, not less than 8 inches, or two courses laid flat.

Hollow concrete blocks or clay tiles: Not less than 8 inches.

Poured concrete or solid concrete blocks: Not less than 4 inches; exposure to severe weather conditions may warrant additional thickness. Poured concrete chimneys require vertical and horizontal lacing of steel reinforcing bars.

Stone: Not less than 12 inches.

Chimney height. In order to draw properly, the chimney must extend at least 3 feet above the roof opening (measured from the uphill side on sloped roofs) and 2 feet above the roof's highest point within 10 feet of the chimney.

At elevations above 2,000 feet, both height of chimney and cross-sectional area of flue should be increased 5 percent for each 1,000 feet of elevation. Consult local building department for detailed figures.

Chimney clearances. An air space must be left between all wood framing members and the outside surface of chimney walls. Clearances may vary, depending on the structural members (studs, beams, joists, girders) and local code requirements, though a 2-inch space is considered standard in most codes. Spaces between chimney and framing are firestopped with metal flashing or strips of metal lath covered with plaster.

Seismic reinforcement. If you live in an area subject to earthquakes, the chimney must be strengthened with vertical reinforcing bars extending the full height of the chimney. Local codes will determine their size, number, and placement. In addition, the chimney must be anchored at each floor or ceiling line unless built completely within exterior walls. For details on anchoring, see "Tying-in the chimney," step 18, page 72.

Spark arresters. Spark-arresting screens are an advisable safety measure, especially in a wooded area. They are required chimney components in some building codes. Use a rust-resistant wire mesh or perforated sheet metal with openings not smaller than 1/2 inch nor larger than 5/8 inch. The top of the screen should be at least 12 inches above the cap.

How to add on a masonry fireplace

The following sequence of steps shows, in a general way, the addition of a simple masonry fireplace to an outside wall. Details may differ from local building codes and practices; if so, follow local guidelines.

1) Laying out the job. Once the fireplace site has been located, mark lines on the outside wall to indicate the opening to be cut. Avoid locating vertical lines directly over wall studs. To locate studs from the outside, either tap the wall with a hammer (the stud responds with a solid thud), measure from a nearby door or window (studs are usually set 16 inches on center), or bore an exploratory hole or two.

Boundaries of the foundation pit are staked out as shown at right. Remember that the foundation must extend at least 6 inches beyond the base of the fireplace structure on all sides.

2) Digging the foundation pit. Dig the foundation pit about 6 inches or so beyond the boundary lines to make room for building concrete forms. The proper depth will depend on frost line depth, soil stability, and local building codes. The sides of the pit should be as vertical as possible, and the pit bottom should be smooth and level. Next, build wood forms to hold wet concrete to the exact outside dimensions of the foundation slab. Place a grid of 1/2-inch reinforcing bars, 12 inches on centers, 5 inches above the bottom of the pit. Support the grid on bricks or scrap 2 by 4 blocks, pulling them out as you pour concrete. For added strength, set four steel rods vertically so they will extend up into the inside corners of the rough brick firebox. (In earthquake areas, rods must extend the full height of the chimney.)

After the concrete is poured it should be allowed to cure. Keep it moist by covering it with damp burlap sacking, polyethylene sheets, or moist earth until fully cured (a week to 10 days).

3) Opening the walls. The next step is to remove the outside wall siding and sheathing to expose the wall and floor framing. Tools and techniques used for this job will depend on the type of material covering the wall. To remove stucco, you'll need a wide mason's chisel and hammer, wire cutters, and nail puller. Wood siding and sheathing may be cut with a hand saw, portable circular saw, or saber saw—or a combination of these.

Remove the siding down to the foundation level. *Do not remove studs*—just clear out everything around them, including cross bracing. Any plumbing or electrical lines will have to be rerouted away from the fireplace.

Next remove the inside wall covering to the dimensions of the opening and use a tarp or thick plastic sheeting to cover the opening while it is exposed.

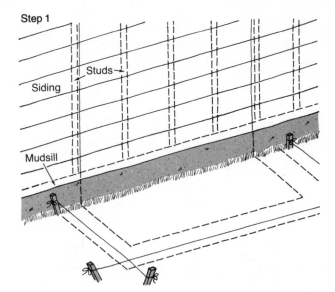

Step 1

Siding
Studs
Mudsill

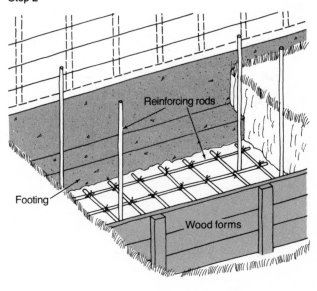

Step 2

Reinforcing rods
Footing
Wood forms

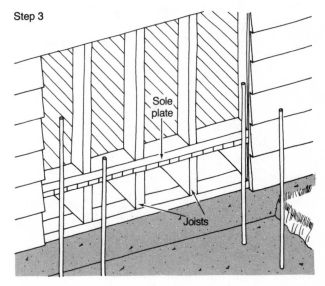

Step 3

Sole plate
Joists

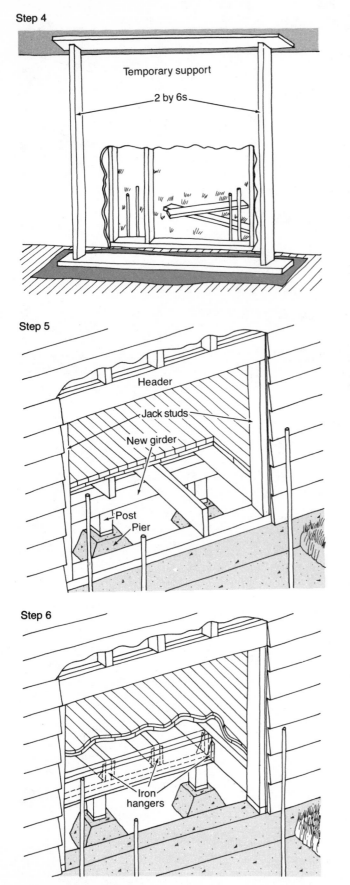

Step 4

Temporary support

2 by 6s

Step 5

Header

Jack studs

New girder

Post
Pier

Step 6

Iron
hangers

4) Cutting the studs. Don't forget that the studs are holding up your roof, as well as keeping the wall in place. Before you cut them, make provision for carrying the load while the wall is open and temporarily weakened.

One way is to transfer the load to a temporary frame made of 2 by 6 uprights and 2 by 8 horizontals. Cut the 2 by 6s about 1/4 inch longer than the measured space, and wedge them between the 2 by 8s. (You may wish to pad the top horizontal to avoid scarring the ceiling.) Be sure to place the frame so it bears weight. If ceiling joists run at right angles to the fireplace wall, there's no problem. If they run parallel to that wall, center the support under the joist nearest the wall, not between two joists.

Once the support is in place, saw the studs through flush with the top of your opening, then install a doubled header of 2 by 6s spaced so that the faces are flush with the edges of adjacent studs. Toenail the trimmed studs to the header. Jack studs are installed to support the header after the floor is opened.

5) Opening the floor. The floor must be removed to the width and depth of the hearth extension. As when removing studs, you will need support for trimmed floor joists, but in this case it will be permanent. Set a 6 by 6 girder under the joists before they are cut, placing it back far enough to allow for the later addition of a doubled header. Support the girder on precast concrete piers and posts. Depending on how much work space you have, you may do this before or after cutting away the flooring.

Once the girder is in place and the flooring is removed, trim the floor joists and cut away the sole plate but not the mudsill. Next, install two jack studs at each side to transfer weight from the header to the mudsill. Save all materials cut away; you may need them to reframe the floor opening. The temporary ceiling support can now be removed.

(If you wish to avoid cutting the floor, plan for a cantilevered elevated hearth—check with your architect and building inspector for details.)

6) Finishing the floor opening. Finish off the floor construction by rebuilding the floor substructure so it can carry the load once borne by the joists you have cut.

First, measure and cut two lengths of 2 by 6 to fit as headers across the exposed ends of the cut joists; butt snugly against the uncut joists on both sides of the opening, and nail firmly in place. End nail the cut joists to the header, or, as an optional step, support the ends of the cut joists in metal hangers as shown.

If uncut joists on either side of the opening are offset from the opening, use pieces cut from joists to support the floor flush with the sides of the opening. Once the floor opening is framed in, remove the section of sill across the bottom of the wall opening, exposing the foundation.

7) Building the ash pit. Now comes the start of the brickwork. Clean all dirt off the top of the concrete foundation slab so the mortar will stick to the slab. Lay a wall two bricks wide across the front and back, one brick wide on the sides. Butt the front wall against the house foundation, making sure the brickwork maintains the required minimum clearance from wood framing and siding.

The two short walls, inside the box, do not have to be locked into the structure. They support the firebox brickwork. The vertical reinforcing rods should be embedded in masonry to protect them from rusting out. Lay bricks diagonally across the corners and fill in with mortar. In most areas, rods need extend only a short distance above hearth level, but in earthquake-prone regions, local codes usually require vertical reinforcing to reach the full height of the chimney.

Be sure to mortar the cleanout door securely in place so embers cannot escape.

8) Forming the subhearth. With the pit finished, it's time to start the subhearth. Keep a wary eye on dimensions to be sure that the surface of the finished hearth comes out flush with the finish flooring. Figure down from the floor surface. Allow for the thickness of the finished hearth material, a bed of mortar (at least 1/2 inch), and at least 6 inches of concrete subhearth under the firebox.

Wooden forms hold the front hearth in place while the concrete is setting, but wood should not be used on the back hearth because it must be removed to conform to code, a nearly impossible task once the subhearth is in place. For the back hearth form, use loose bricks resting on 1/2-inch steel reinforcing rods as shown in the drawing, or use solid brickwork or steel plates. (Some local codes may require that wooden forms be removed from a front hearth as well. If this is the case, be sure you have room to work, or use a metal form.) Remember to provide for an ash dump.

Once the forms are set, place a grid of reinforcing steel 3 inches below the top of the slab and pour the concrete. Use a float to level the surface.

9) Finishing the subhearth. The cut-away drawing shows the finished concrete slab in place. The slab, cantilevered out from the front wall of the ash pit, will be anchored under the weight of brickwork to be laid on the rear hearth.

Any irregularities in the concrete surface should be corrected with mortar when the finished hearth is being laid. (Failure to do so will lead to an uneven firebox floor—not critical, but unsightly and potentially hard to clean.)

Note the placement of the reinforcing steel mat. Vertical steel reinforcing rods are continued through the slab to be cemented in brickwork around the firebox.

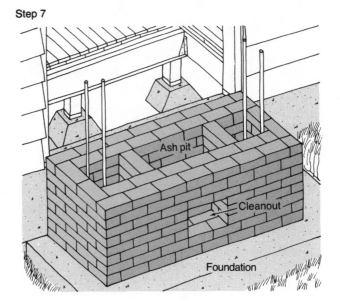

Step 7

Ash pit

Cleanout

Foundation

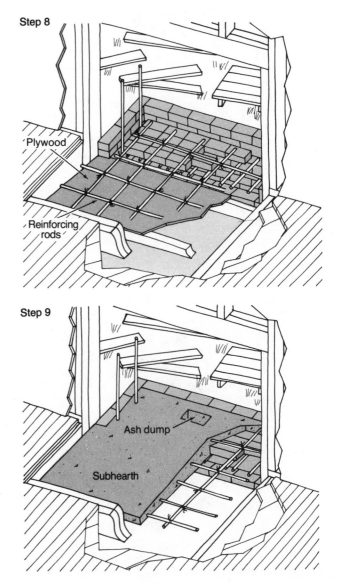

Step 8

Plywood

Reinforcing rods

Step 9

Ash dump

Subhearth

Step 10

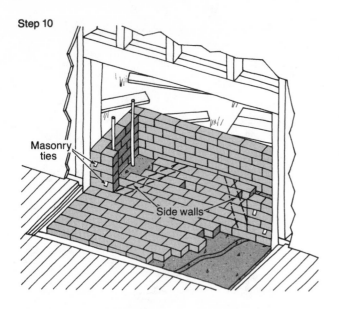

Masonry ties

Side walls

Step 11

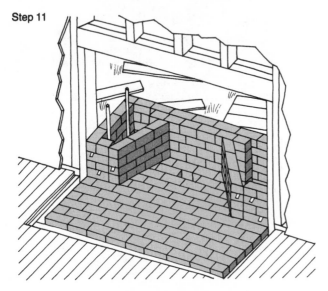

Step 12

10) Finishing the hearth. Lay the inner hearth as soon as the subhearth has had about 12 hours to set and the outer brickwork has been brought up enough courses to reach slightly above finished hearth level. The inner hearth is laid with firebrick, bonded to the subhearth with a 1/2-inch-thick bed of fireclay mortar.

Note that the firebrick floor covers only the area needed for the firebox. When these bricks have been laid, they are usually covered with a layer of sand to protect them from mortar drops as the masonry is built up. The front hearth—usually laid with tile or common brick—can be set at this time or postponed until the facing is laid in place. Note the masonry ties, inserted in the mortar joints, for anchoring the facing when it is attached later. The dotted lines indicate the location of firebox side walls, which always angle inward to improve heat radiation.

11) Laying the firebox. The firebrick walls of the firebox may be laid at the same time as the outer brickwork, or they may be held off until the outer work reaches damper height. Firebricks are laid in a fireclay mortar that has been mixed to consistency of soft butter and applied in a layer 1/8 to 1/4 inch thick. Bricks are laid flat to give greater strength to the wall.

Back and side walls are laid simultaneously, one course at a time. (This must be done because the joints are a complicated set of angles; see step 12.) The space between the angled side walls and the outer brickwork should be filled with broken bricks or other bits and pieces of masonry dropped in loosely to allow for firewall expansion.

12) Setting in the back wall. Lay the back wall plumb for about 12 inches, then slope it forward to reflect heat outward and to provide for a smoke shelf. The angle of slope of this rear wall will be established by the size and height of the fireplace. The slope should form a plane, not a curve. (If the wall is curved, rising currents of warm air will not only flow into the room, they will bring smoke with them.) The rear wall should reach above the level of the lintel, to serve as the back edge of the throat and also as the back bearing surface for the damper.

Since side walls are usually laid to butt against the sloping wall, they have to be beveled at the back end to meet the angle of the wall. One way to cut side walls is to put each course of brick in place dry, hold a straight board (slanted at the proper angle) against the rear edge of the wall, and draw a line along the edge. Disassemble the upper course, cut the rear bricks on the line, and mortar the course into place. After both side walls are laid, the sloping back wall may be mortared in. Tip the first course above the straight wall by making a wedge-shaped joint higher in back than in front.

13) Providing a damper and smoke shelf. Except for smoke domes that both eliminate part of the masonry and have an incorporated damper, dampers fall into two main categories: blade and dome dampers. In the blade type, the damper door is hinged or swiveled in a flat frame. In the dome type (see drawing), the door is fitted into a metal housing shaped into a throat. Some dome dampers, such as the one shown here, are designed with a front edge that serves as lintel for fireplace facing, but most of them simply support the masonry of the inner brickwork. In the latter case, a lintel is installed (to support the facing) after the damper is in position.

Both damper and lintel should have their bearing surfaces at each end wrapped in fiberglass wool to allow for heat expansion.

Dampers come with a choice of controls for opening and closing. Some controls extend through the facing, some work by chain, some have levers operated by a poker.

14) Finishing the facing. With the firebox complete and the damper in place, it is time to build the facing. Don't forget to leave 2 inches of air space between both firebox and facing masonry and the header at the top of the opening. (The building code requires at least 2 inches of clearance between masonry and any combustible material adjacent to the firebox or flue.)

There are several patterns for finishing mortar joints in facings; consult a book on masonry for examples. To obtain smooth mortar joints, use a mason's pointing trowel. It is helpful to practice with it on some rough brickwork first.

Restore the inner wall surface with patching plaster, strips of gypsum board, or whatever material matches the existing surface.

Lay the front hearth to the edges of the subhearth. Fill any gaps with strips of subflooring, then strips of finish flooring salvaged from that removed when you made the floor opening.

15) Sealing around the opening. To make certain that water will not seep into the house around the edges of the fireplace opening, seal all points where masonry passes through the woodwork. Where bricks meet wood framing, they should be laid against felt paper. Around the sides, where masonry meets exterior siding, the joint is flashed or caulked, depending on the type of siding. For stucco walls, use a stucco patch, available at home improvement centers.

Across the top of the firebox, metal flashing is needed to divert water away from the opening. Slip one angle of the flashing under the outer wall covering, cover with weatherproof paper, and then nail on the finished covering. The angle of the flashing that fits into the brickwork should be mortared into a running joint and sealed with mastic. Top flashing is shaped to overlap sides.

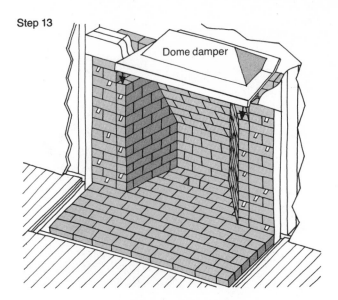
Step 13
Dome damper

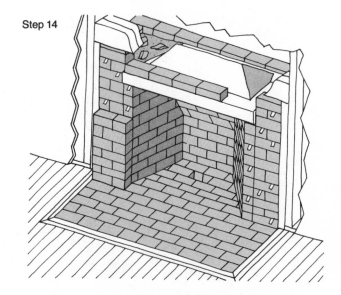
Step 14

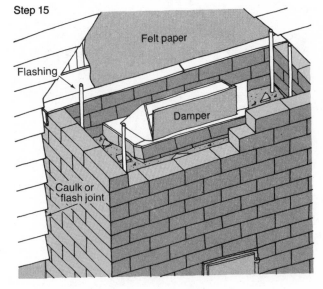
Step 15
Felt paper
Flashing
Damper
Caulk or flash joint

Step 16

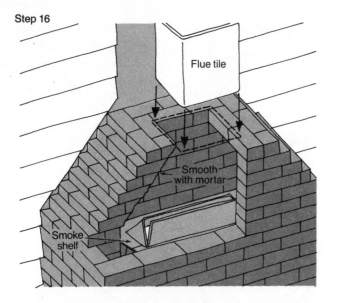

Flue tile

Smooth with mortar

Smoke shelf

Step 17

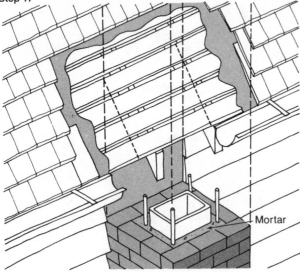

Mortar

Step 18

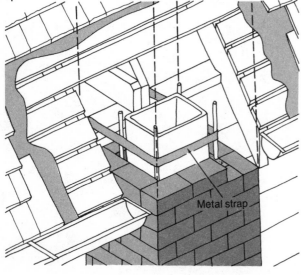

Metal strap

16) Building the throat and chimney. Brickwork on both sides of the firebox should be stepped in for six or seven courses until the throat narrows down to flue size. The last course should be laid to provide a ledge just wide enough for the flue tile to rest upon.

The sloped inner surface—which forms the smoke dome—should be smoothed with mortar to ease the passage of the flue gases and to prevent soot buildup. Mortar used for this job should be slightly richer (more cement, less sand) and drier (less water) than that used for laying brick. Mortar is applied with a square-edged plasterer's trowel. Brick used for the inner surface of the smoke dome should have a textured surface so the mortar will key into it.

Before setting the chimney, fasten weatherproof paper on the house wall where bricks will rest against it. When setting flue tiles, it is more practical to set and cement them in place, then lay the outside bricks around them. (If bricks are laid first, the new masonry is likely to be damaged when the heavy tiles are positioned.) To cut a tile to length, place a cement sack inside, fill tightly with sand, then sever with a series of chisel cuts.

17) Penetrating the roof. At the point where the chimney passes the roof line, it is necessary to cut into the eave in order for the chimney to pass and to install an anchoring device to brace the chimney.

Clear away the shingle or composition roof surfacing for an area a foot larger all around than the opening needed for the chimney.

Mark cutting lines on the roof sheathing 2 inches wider than each side of the masonry and saw out the pieces. Remove enough of the sheathing so you can freely reach the plate. If the tips of the rafters extend beyond the roof line, cut them off flush with the outside wall. If your house is equipped with gutters, cut them with a hacksaw. Note the reinforcing steel in each corner of the chimney masonry, sealed in with mortar. To repeat, this is required only in earthquake country; some local codes ignore it.

18) Tying-in the chimney. The chimney must be anchored to the framing of the house by some means at the point it passes the roof line. There are several ways to do this. The drawing shows one of the most common. A 1-inch iron strap is bent around a tile (and the reinforcing steel, if any), twisted to pass flat through a mortar joint, and nailed to the top plate or to a rafter. If you must fasten to a ceiling joist, nail cross supports across several joists to help distribute the load.

Repair cut gutters by filing off rough edges and soldering caps on each of the cut ends. Be sure to buy caps of the same metal as the gutters; otherwise electrolytic reaction between the different metals will corrode the edges and destroy the seal. (Be sure, too, that there is a downspout to drain each of the severed gutters.)

19) Fitting the flashing. Install metal (copper, lead, galvanized iron, aluminum) flashing around the chimney to seal the opening against water leakage. Flashing is applied in two layers. The bottom layer (B and E in the drawing) is fitted under the roof covering and bent to lie flat against the brickwork. The second layer (A, C, D in the drawing) is cemented and caulked into the masonry and fitted so it overlaps the first layer. This is known as counter flashing.

Except where they overlap, flashing joints should all be soldered. Allow some leeway between cap and base flashing to permit the chimney to settle or move slightly without rupturing the seal. In very cold climates, a cricket (next step) is substituted for flashing on the upside of the chimney.

20) Installing a cricket. In severe winter regions, a cricket or saddle is constructed on the upside of the chimney to divert water and snow away from the top side. Snow and ice collecting against a chimney can seriously damage flashing, resulting in a leaky roof. Heavy snow loads may even do structural damage to the masonry itself.

A sizable cricket consists of a ridgeboard and post, sheathed with plywood or 1-inch boards and covered with sheet metal. Crickets for smaller chimneys may be all sheet metal. Metal flanges extend several inches under shingles and up the chimney. Counter flashing covers the joint where the cricket meets the chimney. You can have the cricket made at a sheet metal shop at the time you order flashing. Install the cricket and counter flashing in the alphabetical sequence shown.

Step 19

Step 20

Cricket

Counterflashing

Plywood or 1" boards

Using a metal insert

Several manufacturers offer metal inserts for masonry fireplaces. These replace the firebox, smoke dome, and damper—saving the complicated work of building the first two and seating the third of these. They also assure correct firebox dimensions and shape for efficient draw in the chimney.

As comparison, using a prefabricated metal insert replaces steps 10 through 13 of our typical installation, as well as the corresponding design work.

Some units are conventional, but a majority are designed to make the fireplace a heat-circulating one. The heat-circulating design shown at right is a composite of several manufacturers' units. As indicated, most inserts incorporate the ducts into the basic shell. (A number of prefabricated built-in fireplaces are designed with flexible ducting; see the drawings on page 75 for comparisons.)

Inserts are available in a range of sizes in both conventional and heat-circulating models. When installed, these units require at least 1 inch clearance between their outer shells and surrounding masonry to allow for heat expansion of the metal firebox.

PREFAB INSTALLATION

A typical prefabricated fireplace installation requires neither the credentials of an architect nor the experience of a veteran contractor. Most freestanding fireplace installations are very simple indeed, needing only small openings in wall or ceiling and roof to permit passage of the chimney. Even built-in units may call for no more than modest framing skills. But this is not to say there are no problems at all. Fireplaces built outside a wall and enclosed in a chase may well be beyond average amateur skills.

For the most part, this chapter is meant to serve as a guide to help you plan your specific installation. The emphasis is on how to shop for a fireplace that will meet your needs and how to work out the detailed design you will need to get a building permit.

If you do elect to install your own fireplace, the key as always is planning and more planning. Whether you opt for a freestanding fireplace or a built-in, a successful job depends on knowing where the fireplace will sit, down to the sixteenth of an inch, and what will happen inside the wall or above the ceiling as a result of the placement. Success also depends on knowing how much of what kinds of material you will need to support the fireplace, and how to organize the project from first measurement to last tap of the hammer...or stroke of the trowel.

To simplify explanations, we have divided this chapter into subsections by type of installation. After some initial general advice, there are separate discussions of built-in and freestanding installations. In addition, we have separated the descriptions of built-in installations into inside-the-wall and outside-the-wall sequences, since the requirements in these two cases are not at all the same. If you still are in the planning stage, look through these sequences to get concrete ideas of the options available to you.

Built-in fireplaces

Almost certainly you will have chosen between a heat-circulating and a conventional built-in fireplace early in the planning stages. But this is only the first question. Dozens of models offer hundreds of options, some of them important to heating efficiency, some of them crucial to a fireplace's capacity to fit into your planned installation, some of them important only as esthetic choices.

Unhappily, planning cannot be as untroubled as we all wish when it centers on an object that is prefabricated—which is to say not adaptable to every whim. There must be a certain amount of taking one step forward and two back, especially if the fireplace is being added to an existing structure. Questions fall both upon the fireplace and upon the structure into which it must fit, and all must be answered before you can buy a built-in without fear of finding out too late that something will not fit your situation.

What's available in fireplaces?

To get the fireplace best suited to your needs, shop as widely as you can. Looking first-hand at what is available is the best teacher, and talking with dealers will raise new questions at every turn. This section asks some of the commoner questions and answers some of them.

Dimensions. Typical built-in fireplaces have firebox openings in the range of 28 to 42 inches wide and 16 to 24 inches high. As noted in the chart on page 11, the size of your room will govern to a considerable degree the size of this opening.

Just as important are the overall dimensions of the fireplace. These will determine—at least in part—whether the fireplace projects fully into the room, is placed entirely outside the wall, or falls somewhere between. Typical outside dimensions for built-in fireplaces range from 38 to 52 inches wide, 23 to 26 inches front to back, and 40 to 58 inches from bottom of firebox to top of smoke dome. In short, there is far more variation in overall size than in firebox opening.

Detailed dimensions may matter even more than overall dimensions if you somehow must work with tight space. For one example, the chimney collar may fall at the center of the front-to-back axis, or it may fall on one side or the other of center. Since chimneys must be at least 2 inches away from combustible materials, the exact location of the chimney collar might allow you to run your chimney as planned in a partially projecting fireplace, or might prohibit you from putting it where you expected.

Similar questions can be raised about duct openings in heat-circulating models, as their placement varies even more widely than that of chimney collars.

Duct placement in heat-circulating fireplaces.
Warm air rises, cold air sinks, so the first rule of duct placement is simple enough: cold air intakes are at or near the bottom of the fireplace, and warm air outlets are at or near the top. Still, manufacturers offer a great variety of placements of both intakes and outlets, and for good reasons.

To decide which placements will work best for you requires a thoughtful appraisal of where you wish the warmed air to go, and a careful look at how the face of the fireplace will relate to duct openings. This is of prime importance if you are looking at models with fixed inlets and outlets, but even models with adjustable ducting have some limitations that may make one unit preferable to others.

For one example, it is difficult or impossible to place an outlet vent lower than the point at which the adjustable portion of the ducting leaves the fireplace shell. In a situation where you wish to get warmed air into the room at the lowest possible elevation in order to get maximum warmth near the fireplace, it will pay to look for models with relatively low outlets.

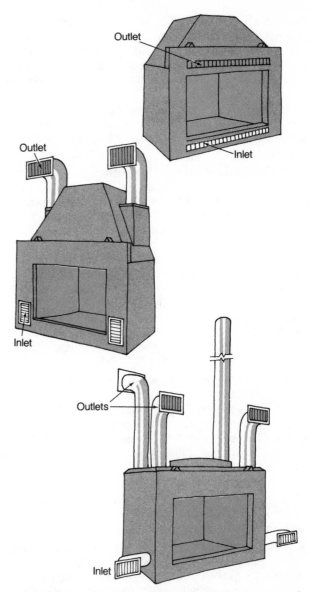

Variations on the theme of heat circulation are several. Units that expel warmed air at the top of the fireplace opening serve best if heat is meant to be kept close to the fireplace; higher outlets send air farther away.

On the other hand, if you want some of the warmed air to rise into a stairwell, or even to be ducted into an upstairs room, you might prefer to look for a unit with ducts placed higher off the floor.

Another point on placement: some models are designed to take air in from the front and expel it from the sides, or vice versa. In others, all vents are in the front. This may be a factor in how you can design your fireplace facing. Corner fireplaces, for example, are easier to frame if all vents are at the front. So are fireplaces set outside a wall.

If you're fighting for space, you may need a fireplace with ducting and vents incorporated into the shell rather than extending out to each side.

Forced air circulation. If a heat-circulating fireplace is to be located in a room of large volume, you may wish to look into low-velocity fans for the ducting. These are built into some luxury models or may be added as options in others. The idea is the same as in a forced air furnace: to mix air evenly rather than let it drift into warmer and cooler layers. Fans may be most valuable in rooms with high ceilings, where warm air tends to rise above head height if it is not kept moving.

Outside air duct for combustion. The heat efficiency of any fireplace is improved by ducting combustion air from outside. As noted in the opening chapter, weathertight houses can inhibit draft too much for a fire to burn well, and draft-ridden houses can even experience a net heat loss as the fire sucks outside air through cracks around doors and windows to feed combustion. The placement of an inlet in a built-in fireplace can be crucial. In some models, the duct is in the firebox floor, so it must reach down into a crawl space or basement. In others, paired ducts at the sides are flexible, so they can reach down through the floor or out through a wall; these add several inches to the width of framing.

Fireclay lining in firebox. All firebox floors are lined with fireclay. In some units, all firebox surfaces are lined. In others, only the back wall may be. In still others, you can buy clip-in side walls to complete the lining. (There is an esthetic choice, too. Some linings are patterned to look like brick; others are smooth surfaced.)

The functional difference is *when* you get warmed, not how much. The fireclay slows the convection process at first, but once heated, it keeps warming air even after the fire dwindles.

Knockout for gas jets. If you plan to have a gas log lighter, placement of the knockouts can be a factor, especially if you will have to work in cramped space or if you plan a partial projection of the fireplace. Most units have knockouts on both side walls.

Weight. Fireplace units alone weigh in the range of 150 to 400 pounds. Class A chimneys 15 inches in diameter weigh about 8 pounds per lineal foot. Since floors are designed to carry dead weight loads of 40 pounds per square foot, these weights are not critical in themselves. However, if you plan to use one of the heavier facings around your fireplace, total weight may require extra under-floor support. You will want to keep accurate measure, especially if the installation is away from a bearing wall.

What's available in chimneys

Built-in fireplaces must be connected to Class A (all fuel) chimneys. To meet codes, these chimneys must be installed with approved supports and other related devices. Use only pipe and components provided or specified by the fireplace manufacturer.

Class A chimneys come in varied lengths (usually 12, 18, 24, 36, and 48 inches) and outside diameters (8, 10, 12, and 15 inches). Which diameter you use will be governed by the collar on top of your fireplace. Lengths usually are mixed in any one installation in order to keep joints away from combustible materials and to allow maximum support. Some dealers offer formulas for mixing lengths.

Most Class A chimneys are designed to allow weather exposure, but some are meant only for use in protected conditions.

Unlike fireplaces, they do not allow zero clearance. In most cases, the walls are 2 inches thick and must have 2-inch clearance from combustible materials all around.

To maintain required clearances in inside installations, manufacturers offer firestop spacers for use when the chimney passes through a ceiling or floor, and flashing for use at the roof. For exterior installations, wall bands serve the same purpose.

Most codes also require that these chimneys be capped as weather protection. A majority of caps double as spark arresters.

Elbows—usually available in 15° and 30° bends—allow offsets in chimneys. For a minor shift, two can be fitted directly together. To accomplish a larger offset, a length of pipe can be sandwiched between a pair.

For situations where a chimney passes through a wall, you will need a thimble—a special type of firestop spacer. There are designs for both horizontal and angled chimneys.

Above the roof, you will need flashing, a storm collar, and a chimney cap for weather protection. Most caps double as spark arresters. In some cases, you may also need bracing.

Measuring for a chimney. To estimate your needs, first make an elevation sketch of your house similar to the one at right. As shown, measure the height of the fireplace room (A), the room above, if any (B), and the attic from the proposed ceiling opening to the high side of the roof opening (C).

Next, figure the chimney height above the roof. The chimney must extend at least 3 feet above the high side of the roof opening, and must also be 2 feet taller than the highest point on the roof within 10 feet of the opening (measured horizontally, as shown). The highest point may be a ridge, dormer, or cupola; on steep-pitched roofs, the point may fall on the roof plane itself. To get the total height, add the above-roof height to measurements A, B, and C, plus the thicknesses of ceilings and roof.

To determine the amount of chimney pipe needed, subtract from your original total the height of the fireplace, and that of a raised hearth if you're using one. Note any offsets.

This information will allow your fireplace dealer

Measuring for a chimney

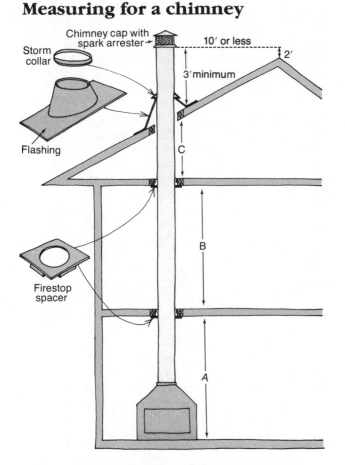

Chimney cap with spark arrester
Storm collar
Flashing
Firestop spacer
10' or less
2'
3' minimum
C
B
A

to help you estimate your chimney material requirements. (A reminder: You probably will need variable lengths of pipe for the safest, sturdiest chimney; a dealer's advice can be helpful.)

Building in a built-in

Where you put the fireplace in relation to a wall—or walls—does much to govern the size of the job.

As shown in the drawing on page 10, the basic choices are to place the fireplace inside a wall or to fit it through a wall. If you place the unit inside a wall, structural alterations in an existing building are limited to cutting through the ceiling and roof for passage of the chimney, but you lose a maximum of interior space. If you fit the fireplace through an outside wall, structural alterations include opening the wall and probably cutting through an eave, but you are repaid in saved space. Fitting the fireplace into an interior wall is a possibility not to be overlooked if you have space to spare in a room adjoining the one where you wish to put the fireplace.

In addition to structural alterations, you must add framing to cover the sides and back of the fireplace and part or all of the chimney. Interior framing is less critical than exterior because inside work does not have to withstand weathering and require foundation.

Space or other factors may force you to ac worst of all possible compromises, a firepla⟨ is half inside, half outside, and so in need ol ⟨⟨⟨⟨ indoor and outdoor framing as well as the more difficult structural changes.

The sequences on pages 78–83 show in some detail the steps involved in typical inside and outside installations.

Once you have made your basic site selection using the factors outlined on pages 10–13, you will need to pinpoint fireplace placement with your specific structural limitations in mind. Most of these are obstructions to passage of the chimney. As noted in the section on chimney components (page 76), designs are available that will allow you to run the chimney inside or outside, or—by offsetting it to pass through a wall— some of each.

Estimating building materials

To get a clear picture of how much a fireplace will cost, you will need to make an estimate of building materials.

Framing lumber for the fireplace and raised hearth is usually 2 by 4 for top and sole plates and studs. In most cases, framing inside the house is covered by 3/8-inch gypsum board or plywood if the final facing is to be of masonry. Facing also may match existing interior walls.

For a fireplace installed inside, headers at openings in ceilings and roof should match existing joists and rafters. If extra support is required under the floor, this support, too, should match existing members.

For fireplaces installed outside an exterior wall, headers for opened walls must be 2 by 6. The chase enclosing fireplace and chimney must have a masonry foundation and conventional 2 by 4 stud walls. Chases usually are covered to match exterior walls, but may be faced with simulated masonry or masonry veneer. Most chases are insulated all or in part with fiberglass batts to protect the fireplace against heat loss.

If you are not familiar with these terms, or with the specifics of construction, let the descriptions of typical installations on pages 78–83 guide you in making estimates of the materials you will need.

The tools you need

The framing tools include hammer, saw(s), carpenter's square, spirit level, plumb line, drill and bits, slot and Phillips screwdrivers, and a good measuring tape.

For masonry work, the basic tools are trowel, float, and brick set or tile cutter, plus a mixing bucket.

You should not need sheet metal tools, except, perhaps, for tin snips to trim flashing.

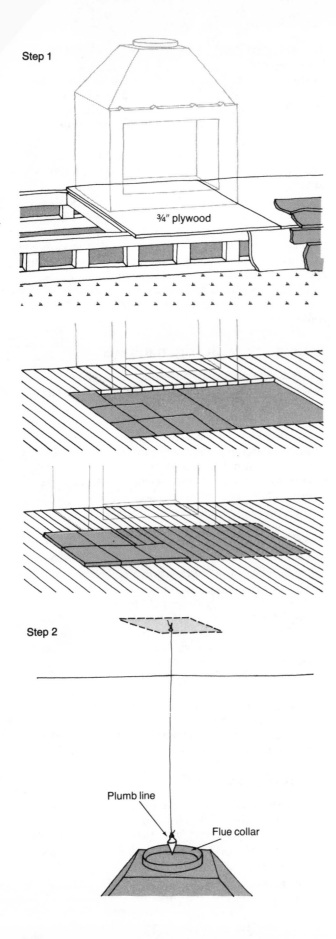

Step 1

¾" plywood

Step 2

Plumb line

Flue collar

Installing a built-in—inside a wall

The following step-by-step sequence shows a typical installation. It is meant only as a general planning guide to help you work out details of your installation, and help you decide whether you wish to do the work or hire it done.

1) Locate and prepare hearth site. With the fireplace location precisely established and marked, the hearth site must be prepared before you place the fireplace in position. You have three basic options: raised hearth, hearth flush with floor, and hearth laid over finished floor.

For a raised hearth, frame a platform over the finished floor. The technique shown for the vertical sections is the same as for a stud wall. Use 3/4-inch plywood for the platform. Reinforce the platform with 2 by 4 cross members centered beneath joints in the plywood. Remember that the bottom thickness of the firebox of a zero clearance fireplace ranges from 6 to 9 inches, so the opening will be noticeably higher than the hearth extension unless you set the fireplace on a separate, lower platform.

For a hearth extension flush with the finished floor, cut away the finished floor to the desired width and length. The noncombustible hearth materials must be a minimum 3/8 inch thick and without a break, and must cover a code-required minimum area. Most finished floors are 3/8 inch or thicker, but almost none is thick enough to allow hearth and hearth extension to meet flush.

For a hearth laid over a finished floor, no carpentry is required, but note that such hearths produce a toe-stubbing lip, and thick ones may obstruct inlets of a heat-circulating fireplace.

Do not lay the forehearth at this time.

With help from a friend, move the fireplace into its exact position. Secure it against movement with temporary blocks nailed at each side and—if the fireplace stands away from the wall—at each rear corner.

2) Locate and cut ceiling opening. To find the center of the ceiling opening for a vertical chimney, plumb to the center of the fireplace chimney collar as shown. If the chimney is to be offset, plumb as shown, then use the formula provided by the manufacturer to transfer the center point.

The opening is cut square, with two sides parallel to the ceiling joists; it must be 4 inches wider than the diameter of the chimney pipe. If you're working into an unfloored attic, the single opening is enough. If you're working toward a floor above, you will have to cut through it. You can cut either a matching square hole, or a circle 4 inches larger in diameter than the chimney. In this case, use a scout drill to mark the center of the top opening by drilling through both ceiling and floor.

3) Frame ceiling opening. With an opening for the chimney cut in the ceiling, one joist will obstruct the opening if you are using chimney pipe with a standard outside diameter of 15 inches and your joist spacing is a standard 16 inches on center. If this is the case, and you're working into an unfloored attic, work from above.

First, tack temporary supports across the joist to be trimmed and its neighbors on either side. Then trim out the joist that obstructs the opening, allowing room for doubled headers at each side. Using lumber of the same dimensions as the joists, install these doubled headers. You can nail into the ends, or toenail. Either way, use at least two nails at each end of each header, and two to secure the trimmed joist end. Add single crosspieces to make a square frame around the opening.

If there is a finished floor above, or if you're working toward a flat roof having no crawl space between it and the ceiling, you won't have to brace before you trim out the obstructing joist, but you will have to enlarge the ceiling opening to accommodate the doubled headers and crosspieces. (If you're planning a close-fitting framing around the chimney, you may have to patch the edges of your opening, but in most cases the framing will more than cover the opening.) Fit the headers from below, toenailing them into place; then add the crosspieces. It will help to have opened the floor or roof above before you begin framing, so a helper can steady the members while you nail. (On occasion, you may be able to nail from the roof, but avoid the temptation to make this the larger opening; it will make flashing more difficult to install.)

4) Install firestop spacer. A firestop spacer assures the code-required 2-inch minimum clearance between the chimney and combustible materials on all sides, and one must be used each time a chimney penetrates a ceiling or floor. If you can work from above, it is best to install the firestop spacer on top of the ceiling joists. If you don't have access, nail it to the bottom edges of the joists.

In those cases where joists (or rafters) support both ceiling and roof, the roof flashing (see drawing, page 80) takes the place of the firestop spacer.

5) Assemble chimney sections. Once the firestop spacer is in place, begin assembling the chimney sections. Most fireplace manufacturers provide a special starter section that locks into the collar at the top of the fireplace. Above this, regular sections fit together with some sort of twist and lock motion.

You may find it helpful to practice fitting two sections together at floor level, where there is less strain and visibility is better. Upper ends usually are marked with an arrow or the word "up" to avoid any chance of the chimney being installed upside down.

Continue upward only until the chimney extends just slightly beyond the firestop spacer or the flashing.

Step 3

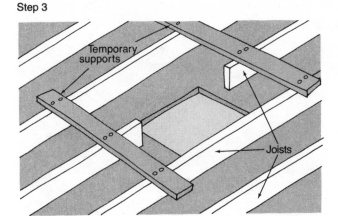

Step 4

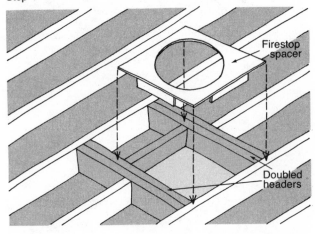

Step 5

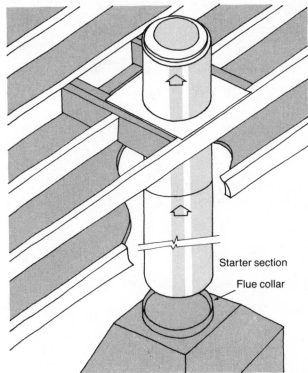

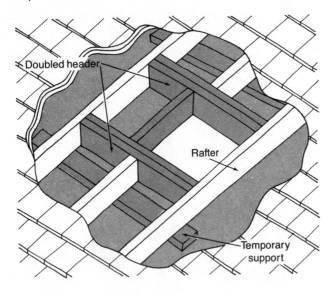

Doubled header

Rafter

Temporary support

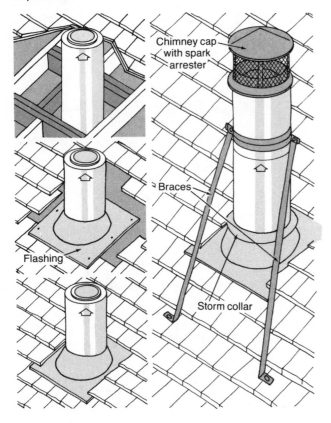

Chimney cap with spark arrester

Braces

Flashing

Storm collar

6) Locate and cut roof opening. The process for locating the center point of the roof opening is exactly the same as that shown for finding a ceiling opening (see step 2, page 78), except that you plumb to the center of the chimney section where it extends above the firestop spacer. If the chimney run is straight, drive a nail through the roof to mark the point. If you plan to offset the chimney, use the manufacturer's formula to locate the center of the opening.

Measure and mark the opening from atop the roof. On a pitched roof, it will have to be oblong to provide the required 2 inches of clearance on all sides of the chimney. Cut from on top of the roof.

7) Frame roof opening. When rafters are spaced 16 inches on centers, the process is very similar to framing the ceiling opening, except that—where a roof rafter must be trimmed—temporary braces are tacked on from the underside. Use doubled headers of the same dimension lumber as the rafters to support each end of the trimmed rafter, and single members to frame the remaining sides.

In many houses, rafters are spaced more than 16 inches on centers, so you may be able to avoid trimming one, though it's possible you'll need to make an offset with a pair of elbows. (In planning, you may wish to locate the offset between the fireplace and the ceiling, where there usually is more room to maneuver than there is in the attic. Obviously, it is too late to do this after the ceiling opening has been cut and framed.)

No firestop spacer is required at the roof; the flashing serves in its place.

8) Install flashing and storm collar. Manufacturers vary in their approach to flashing. Some require that it be installed before the chimney is extended upward through the roof opening; others use designs that can be placed after the chimney pokes through the roof. Most often it's a matter of how the flashing fits under the roofing. In any event, pay strict heed to the installation instructions provided by the manufacturer of your chimney.

Once the flashing is in place and the chimney extended above it, place the storm collar over the chimney pipe and push it down snug against the flashing. Seal the joint between storm collar and chimney pipe with a waterproof caulk or mastic.

Note: This instruction assumes the chimney will remain exposed above the roof. If you choose to enclose it, check with your building department for code requirements on framing and other construction details.

9) Cap chimney and brace. Once the chimney has been assembled to its full height, fit the cap to its top. Chimneys extending 5 feet or more above the roof may be required to have bracing. Check with your building department or dealer. The bracing shown meets most codes.

10) Frame in fireplace. Enclose the fireplace as you would frame a conventional wall. Typically, this means using 2 by 4s for sole and top plates, and 2 by 4s spaced 16 inches on centers for studs. Some local building codes permit 2 by 3s as studs in nonbearing walls such as these, but check with your building department before buying your lumber.

If you're installing a heat-circulating fireplace with flexible ducting, you will have to frame openings for inlets or outlets, or both. You may wish to make a trial assembly of the ducts before framing begins, to make sure they will fit the framing without problems. Also, before you begin to frame, cut the opening for an outside combustion air duct and plumb the gas line for a gas log lighter if you are using these optional devices.

The framing members must be set back from the front edge of the firebox opening so that facing materials will fit as you plan. If you will leave the fireplace face frame exposed, set the studs back far enough for the facing to fit flush with the frame. (For example, if you're using 3/8-inch gypsum board, set the framing 3/8 inch behind the face frame. If you plan to cover the wall framing with standard brick, the offset must equal the brick plus 3/8 inch for the gypsum board or plywood skin covering the framing plus the thickness of the mortar between brick and skin.)

Standard finish for the face frame of most built-in units is black-painted metal. If you cover this with tile or other masonry, the framing must be adjusted to compensate for the covering material.

The drawings show framing details for typical corner, flush, and projecting fireplace installations.

11) Facing fireplace. The variations of material and technique are too numerous to explain in detail. However, two basic rules apply.

If you're using plywood, gypsum board, or any other combustible material for facing, it must not cover the face frame. It must butt flush against the outer edges of the frame, or, if it is to project forward beyond the face frame, it must be set at least 6 inches from the sides of the firebox opening and 12 inches above the top. This requirement applies also to mantels and mantel shelves.

If your facing material weighs heavily—as a stone or adobe block wall—the flooring beneath may have to be reinforced. Your building department will recommend a specific structure.

For more information on installing masonry, you may wish to consult the *Sunset* books *Walks, Walls & Patio Floors* and *Remodeling with Tile.*

12) Finish forehearth. The hearth extension must be covered with a noncombustible material at least 3/8 inch thick. The extension must be continuous: tile must be grouted, brick mortared. You can lay masonry loose only if you underlay it with 24-gauge sheet metal.

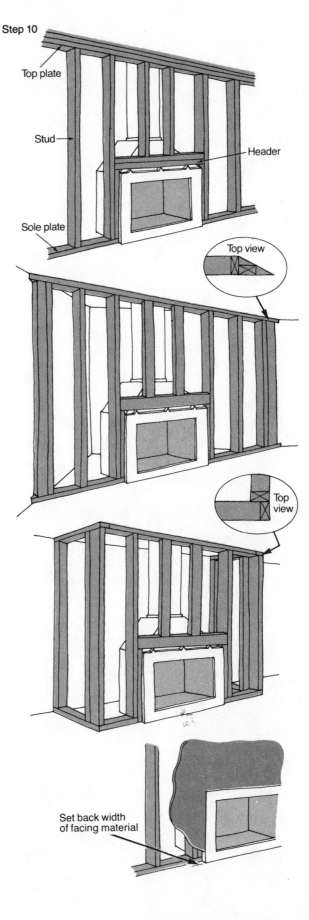

Step 10

Top plate

Stud

Header

Sole plate

Top view

Top view

Set back width of facing material

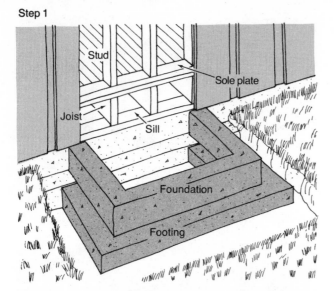

Step 1

Step 3

3/4" plywood

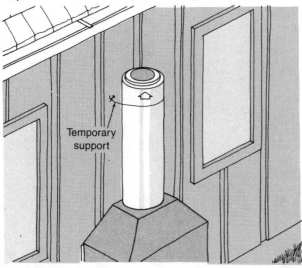

Step 5

Temporary support

Installing a built-in—outside a wall

Common building practice dictates that outside fireplace installations be enclosed completely within a chase—a sort of room without windows or doors. The chase both protects and hides the metal firebox and chimney. A chase can narrow above the fireplace and be covered to resemble a masonry chimney, or it can extend in an unbroken line to the top and be covered to match the siding of the house. In either case, adding the framing to an existing building is complex. Skilled amateurs can do the work, but most homeowners prefer to hire a contractor. The following sequence describes a typical installation, but it is only a guide to planning, not an instruction.

1) Build foundation. Measure and dig out the site to receive a continuous footing and foundation of the same size as those of your house. To meet typical building codes, the foundation will have steel reinforcing bars not only within itself, but tying it to the existing foundation. Top the foundation with a mudsill. (Typically, the mudsill will be flush with its counterpart in the main foundation, but the foundation is one opportunity to control the height of the platform on which the fireplace will rest. See step 3.)

2) Open wall. This is a complex operation. First, cut away both interior and exterior wall surface materials. Next, erect a support reaching from floor to ceiling and beyond each side of the opening. (This supports ceiling joists once you cut wall studs. See the sequence for adding a masonry fireplace, page 68, step 4.)

With the ceiling support in place, trim out wall studs blocking the opening. Nail in a doubled header of 2 by 6s, then add two jack studs at each side. Once the jack studs are in place, trim out the sole plate if you are planning a forehearth flush with the inside finished floor, the usual case in this space-saving installation.

3) Frame platform for fireplace. The drawing here assumes a platform flush with the inside *subfloor,* permitting a 3/8-inch-thick forehearth that will be flush with the finished floor. In this case, you can overlap (plate) joists for the platform with existing joists in your subfloor. To plate, overlap the extension joist at least a foot along the existing floor joist, and secure with at least three nails at each end of the overlap. It is best to nail from both sides.

If you plan to change level (in order to have a raised hearth, or to lower the fireplace so the firebox floor is flush with the hearth extension), consult with your building department before designing a foundation and joist system. Especially in cases of lowering a firebox, you risk violating codes on minimum clearance of wood from earth, and minimum clearance of wood from firebox opening.

4) Position fireplace. With the platform complete, slide the fireplace into position, then add a sole plate around the platform perimeter.

5) Assemble chimney. Chimney sections lock together. If you are using 15-inch-diameter pipe, assemble it at least to eave height before you begin to frame, because such pipe will not fit between studs set 16 inches on centers. It is a good idea to hold the pipe in place with temporary wire bands while you frame. Smaller diameters of pipe can be assembled at this point or after framing is complete.

6) Cut away eave. To accommodate the framing for the chase, cut the eave line back flush with the house wall, and just wide enough to accept the framing plus its covering. (For a more complete description of this step, again see the sequence for adding on a masonry chimney, page 72, steps 17–18.)

7) Frame chase. This is the difficult task for many amateur carpenters. The basics are straightforward enough: use 2 by 4 studs to the desired height, spacing them 16 inches on centers and anchoring them to sole and top plates. Diagonal bracing maybe required by code, but this is simple, too. The complications arise in securing the studs butted against the existing wall to framing members inside that wall, in narrowing the chase if this is part of the design, and in installing flashing where the side walls of the chase meet the existing walls of the house. If you're not familiar with the techniques, seek professional advice.

Another area of some complexity is fireblocking. One fireblock is required for each 8 feet of vertical rise. These fireblocks must form a solid horizontal stop across the chase to block upward drafts, and the chimney must have a firestop spacer where it passes through the fireblock, as in inside installations. Our drawing approximates the framing for a code-approved firestop, but you should check with your building inspector before designing your chase. The horizontal cover usually is 5/8-inch plywood. (The cover is not shown in the drawing; it must fit snug against the chase walls on all four sides, meeting firestop blocks set between the studs.)

8) Close chase and cap chimney. When the chase reaches its full height, install a closing (prefabricated sheet metal closures are usually available in several sizes from fireplace dealers) and then cap the chimney itself, using a manufactured cap matched to the chimney.

9) Insulate and cover chase. Chases should be insulated with R-11 or thicker fiberglass batts. In mild climates, the insulation need enclose only the fireplace; in severe winter areas, the whole chase should be insulated. Covering may match the house or simulate masonry.

10) Frame and face fireplace. The options are many. For more explanation, see the sequence for an inside installation (page 81, step 10) and also page 14.

Step 6

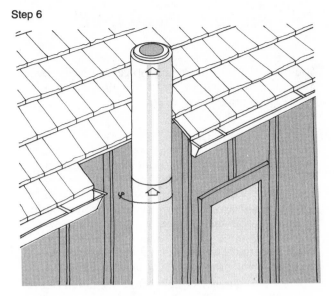

Step 7

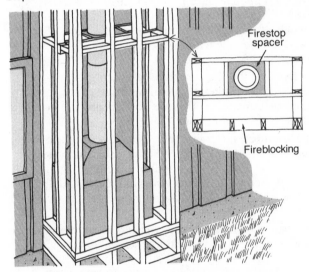

Firestop spacer

Fireblocking

Steps 8 and 9

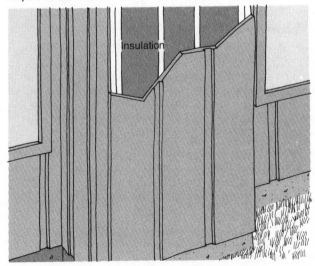

Insulation

Freestanding metal fireplaces

Of all the fireplaces, these are the easiest to install. You move the unit in like an appliance, place it over a noncombustible floor hearth, install the chimney, then connect the two with stove pipe.

What's available

Even after you take into account all of the sculptured shapes, freestanding prefabricated fireplaces come in a surprising variety of designs. Some types closely resemble wood stoves. Others, heat-circulating models, much resemble their built-in cousins. Still, the vast majority are ultramodern designs with almost as much decorative as practical value. The drawings on page 7 typify this latter school of thought.

A few of the major design factors are noted below.

Finishes. A majority of freestanding fireplaces are finished in enamel or porcelain enamel, with every part of the color spectrum represented. (These usually are bought with matching stove pipe.) For more conservative tastes, there are units finished in traditional stove black.

Because the finish replaces the facing of masonry on built-in fireplaces, careful selection of shape and color is imperative. There is no changing the face of these freestanding units.

Dimensions. Heights of freestanding fireplaces are as variable as their shapes. Some globular models reach only 30 to 35 inches above the floor, while extreme conical designs tower as much as 90 inches. An average unit falls in the neighborhood of 40 to 45 inches.

Diameters of globes or cylinders range between 24 and 48 inches, as do widths of stovelike rectangular models. The smaller types take wood up to 20 inches long; larger ones will accept 27 to 30-inch sticks.

Most freestanding fireplaces rest on the floor, on pedestals, but a few are designed to be suspended.

Weight. Typical units weigh in the range of 140 to 150 pounds. Lightweights go as low as 90 pounds; heavyweights approach 400.

The reason for the generally light weights of freestanding fireplaces is that typical units have single metal walls to enhance heat radiation. Heavier freestanding fireplaces are heat-circulating models with double walls, ducting, and other extras attached.

Many single-wall models come without a refractory liner in place in the firepit; the unit comes instead with a bag of dry fireclay. Buyers mix their own mortar and form their own lining. Manufacturers supply precise instructions if this is the case.

Heat-circulating fireplaces. A few deluxe freestanding fireplaces circulate heated air through ducting systems. One circular model has inlets around the base of its pedestal and an outlet across the top of the firebox opening. A rectangular unit has inlets at the rear and outlets on either side of the firebox opening. Both have small fans to force air circulation.

Some units also are fitted with ducts to bring combustion air from outside. (Only fireplaces with this capability are approved for use in mobile homes.)

Installing the fireplace itself is a breeze.

Installation instructions provided by the fireplace manufacturer include hearth requirements, recommended distances between fireplace and combustible surfaces, and details on chimney installation. A few freestanding metal fireplaces have zero clearance requirements and can be placed directly against a combustible wall; clearance distances required for other models range from 6 to 36 inches from combustibles. All must have floor hearths to protect combustible floors from flying sparks and embers.

Several freestanding models are designed to be suspended from the ceiling. Chains used to suspend them must be anchored firmly to ceiling joists as specified by the manufacturer. Like all the others, suspended fireplaces must have hearths.

Building the hearth

Hearths for freestanding fireplaces can be made of almost any noncombustible material, though brick, stone, and tile are most often used. Floor hearths may be raised or installed flush with the finished flooring. They should be level to assure proper chimney connections.

The size of the hearth will depend on the size and shape of your fireplace and the required distance the hearth must extend beyond the fireplace opening. For fireplace openings smaller than 6 square feet, the hearth must extend 16 inches in front of the opening and 8 inches beyond each side of the opening. Openings 6 square feet or larger require hearth extensions 20 inches in front of and 12 inches beyond each side of the opening.

Hearth materials must be at least 3/8 inch thick, and one element of the hearth must be continuous. Without a noncombustible underlay, brick and stone must be mortared, or tile grouted. If you prefer to lay the masonry loose, then you must cut and lay a sheet of 24-gauge sheet metal and place the masonry on top of it. Do not lay a hearth over carpeting.

Often when a fireplace is located near a wall or in a corner, the hearth is extended up the wall for decorative purposes. But applying a noncombustible hearth material to the wall doesn't mean you can reduce the recommended clearance distance from the fireplace to the wall. In order to reduce clearances safely, you must insulate the wall according to the requirements set forth by your local building department, regardless of what material is on the surface.

Variations on installing a chimney

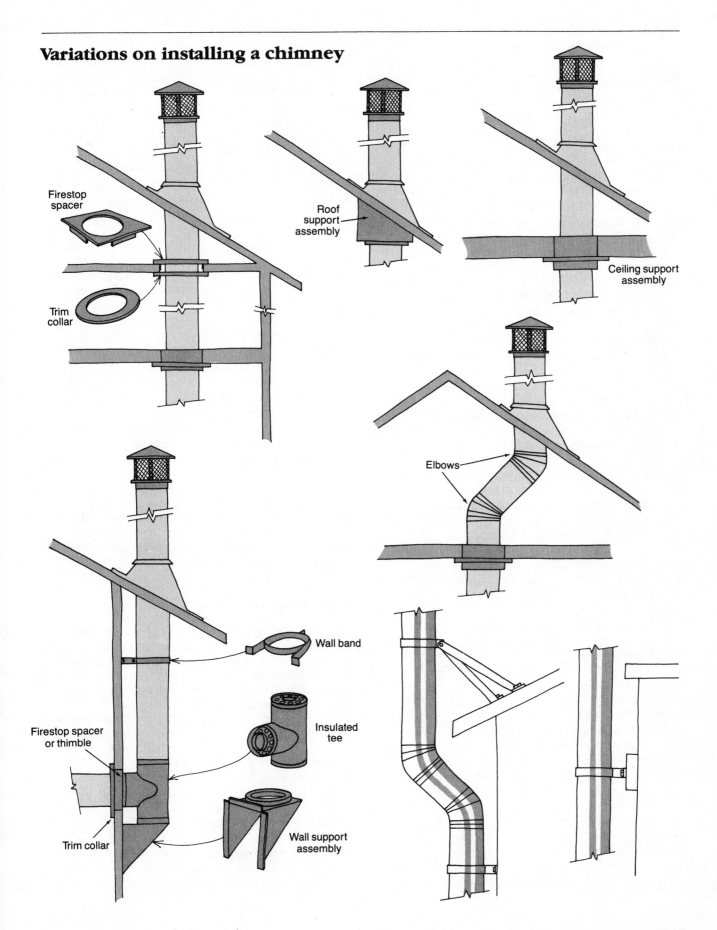

Firestop spacer

Trim collar

Roof support assembly

Ceiling support assembly

Elbows

Wall band

Insulated tee

Firestop spacer or thimble

Trim collar

Wall support assembly

Attractive hearth designs for freestanding metal fireplaces appear on pages 44–47.

Installing the chimney

Chimneys for freestanding metal fireplaces start at the wall or ceiling. You can install a prefabricated metal chimney for the fireplace, or if your house has an existing, unused flue, you can use it (see "Using existing chimneys," page 87).

Prefabricated metal chimneys for freestanding fireplaces and wood stoves must be of Class A pipe; such pipe and its related fittings have been tested for safety and approved by Underwriter's Laboratories (UL), and are code approved. You cannot use single-wall pipe or vent pipe intended for gas or oil-burning appliances. Single-wall pipe never should pass through walls or ceilings. It is used only in the same room as the fireplace to connect it to the chimney. Your fireplace dealer can help you choose suitable pipe and chimney components, and can either provide them or recommend a source.

Chimney installation techniques for freestanding fireplaces are similar to those for built-in fireplace chimneys. The major difference is that instead of the chimney being supported by the fireplace, as in built-in installations, the chimney is supported by the wall or ceiling where it enters the room. In addition to standard prefabricated chimney components (pipe, elbows, firestop spacers, roof flashing, and chimney cap), the installation will require a chimney support assembly.

Support assemblies include all components required to support the weight of the chimney. They're available prefabricated for wall-supported chimneys, roof (rafter) supported chimneys, and ceiling (joist) supported chimneys. All approved support assemblies are designed to provide the required clearance where the chimney passes through a combustible wall or ceiling.

Other components you may need include wall bands (braces) to support the chimney up an outside wall, metal braces to support the chimney above the roof, and trim collars to cover holes where the chimney passes through walls and ceilings. Several common chimney installations and their components appear on page 85.

Installation tips. Manufacturers of prefabricated metal chimneys provide detailed installation instructions which should be read in advance, then followed to the letter, because pipe assembly and component installation will vary with each manufacturer. However, some general pointers can help in the planning.

First, determine where the chimney will run and what components will be needed for the installation. Note the guidelines given on page 76 under "What's available in chimneys," then refer to the installations on page 85 to see which one best suits your situation.

Next, cut a hole in the wall or ceiling and frame in for the chimney support assembly. If you are using 12-inch pipe or larger, you frame the opening for a ceiling or roof support assembly in the same way that you frame in for a firestop spacer above a built-in fire place (see page 79, step 4).

Support assemblies for smaller freestanding fireplace chimneys (10 inches or less in diameter) will fit between joists or rafters. If chimney location allows, these framing members will not have to be cut.

Next, install the support assembly as the manufacturer instructs and connect the first section of insulated pipe to it. Then, to install the remainder of the chimney, follow steps 6–9 on page 80.

For wall-supported chimneys, the support assembly consists of an insulated "tee," firestop spacer, and support bracket. These you install according to manufacturer's instructions. Next, assemble pipe sections, using wall bands for support at required intervals.

Wall-mounted chimneys either penetrate the roof through the eave, or bypass it, depending on the width of the eave.

If the eave is wide enough, the simplest and easiest method is to cut through, as shown in the illustration on page 85, using flashing to support the chimney.

If the eave is too narrow for this, you have two basic options. In cases where the roof overhang is narrower than the outside diameter of the pipe, use a telescoping tee to set the chimney away from the wall far enough to clear the eave by 2 inches, and use spacer blocks nailed to the wall as anchors for the wall bands, as shown. But if the roof overhang is as wide as or wider than the outside diameter of the pipe, use 15° elbows to offset the chimney. In both cases, the section above the eave line must be braced as shown in the drawings of outside-the-wall installations on page 85.

The chimney connection

The drawing, page 87, shows several ways a freestanding fireplace can be connected to a chimney. The connector pipe is single-wall, 24-gauge stove pipe (available from building suppliers or wood stove dealers) or connector pipe (supplied by the fireplace manufacturer). The latter is usually painted to match the color of the fireplace. Most freestanding fireplaces require a flue damper to control the amount of air feeding the fire. You can buy pipe with a damper built in; this should be the first section of connector pipe above the fireplace.

Most codes require a clearance distance of 18 inches between single-wall connector pipe and combustible walls and ceilings. Horizontal runs of pipe must slope upward from the fireplace at least 1/4 inch per running foot. Horizontal runs should be kept as short as possible and should not exceed 75 percent of the chimney height above the support as-

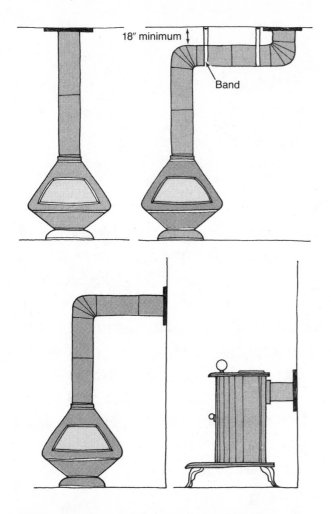

18″ minimum

Band

sembly. Long horizontal runs of pipe do radiate more heat into the room than short ones, but in doing so, they lower flue temperatures, restricting draft and resulting in a smoky fireplace.

Too many bends or turns in the connector pipe also restrict draft. A straight, vertical run directly from the fireplace to the chimney, or a short horizontal run from the fireplace to a wall-supported chimney provides the least restriction of draft. In any case, the chimney connection should have no more than two 90° bends between the fireplace and the support assembly.

Both horizontal and vertical runs longer than 6 feet should have external support. Hangers and wall braces are available from the chimney manufacturer.

Using existing chimneys

Many an older home has an unused masonry chimney that was blocked off when a wood, oil, or coal-burning stove was removed. Fireplaces, too, were blocked off when more modern heating systems were installed. And more recent homes were designed with an extra flue for venting a future stove or fireplace.

If your house has any of these, you may be able to use it for your freestanding fireplace. But it must meet the following requirements:

1) It must have a fireclay flue liner at least 5/8 inch thick.

2) It must be in good repair.

3) If the chimney has an opening into a room, the metal or fireclay thimble must provide adequate clearance from a combustible wall and otherwise meet local codes. The thimble should also be of equal or greater diameter than the connector pipe used for the fireplace. (If the chimney opening does not have a thimble, or if the thimble is the wrong size, you'll have to install one.)

4) The diameter of the chimney flue must be equal to or greater than the diameter of the connector pipe.

Have the chimney checked for all of these factors by a professional mason, a chimney sweep, or the local fire department. In older chimneys, the fireclay flue liners can develop cracks, and mortar between bricks and flue liners can deteriorate—conditions that cause fires. If the chimney needs repairs, get an estimate from a mason. You may find it cheaper to install a new prefab metal chimney than to fix the existing masonry one. If the chimney needs cleaning, have it cleaned before venting the fireplace into it.

When you vent a connector pipe into an existing chimney, be certain the pipe is flush with the inside surface of the flue liner (drawing below). If the connector pipe projects into the flue, it will restrict the draft. To improve draft, block off the chimney flue 8 to 10 inches below the point where the connector pipe enters the chimney, as shown in the drawing. Typically, the block is sheet metal crimped to stay in place through tension. You can use mortar to seal the edges.

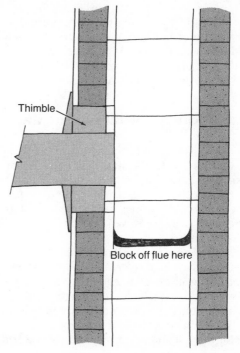

Thimble

Block off flue here

WOOD STOVES

Around the turn of the century, the once-prevalent wood stove was all but abandoned in favor of the more efficient fossil-fueled heaters. In recent years, though, the venerable woodburners have been making a comeback, and today you'll find a wide variety of these stoves on the market—from authentic reproductions of the potbelly stove and cooking range, to modern thermostatically controlled wood-burning heaters designed for contemporary decor.

Where wood is readily available, many people are finding wood stoves and heaters an effective alternative to costly conventional heat. In addition to the savings, there is the nostalgic charm of firing up a grand old parlor stove or preparing a meal on a wood-burning range.

The basic kinds...what's in the name

Stoves come in all shapes and sizes, and the name can tell you a lot about the stove: appearance, traditional location in the house, method of operation, origin of the design, or the name of the manufacturer. The box and potbelly stoves, for example, look the part. Kitchen and parlor stoves traditionally heated kitchens and parlors.

Often, stoves are simply identified as "heating" or "cooking" stoves and referred to by brand name. Heat-circulating stoves and heaters are named for the way they work, drawing cold air in between the inner firebox and outer metal jacket and expelling warmed air. A zero clearance stove is one that requires no spacing between it and a combustible surface and,

unlike other stoves, can be placed directly against a wall. The Scandinavian stove was named for the origin of its design.

A selection of the classic stove types is shown on the opposite page.

...& how they work

Unlike fireplaces, wood stoves work on the principle of controlled combustion. By regulating the airflow into the stove, you control the burning rate and hence the heat output. Modern "airtight" stoves are sealed tight except for one or two adjustable air inlets or dampers that direct air precisely where it's needed for efficient combustion. These dampers are either manually operated or controlled by a thermostat. Properly loaded, many airtight stoves will hold a fire up to 12 hours without reloading. They may also be left unattended during this time without danger of sparks or embers flying out into the room.

Most older stoves are not airtight. The amount of air flowing into these stoves through unintentional as well as intentional openings is usually controlled by a damper located in the stovepipe.

Choosing the right stove

Before you buy any stove, consult your local building department. There are two good reasons to do this—in most communities, the stove and its installation must pass a building inspection; in addition, your building department will offer guidelines for planning a safe stove installation. A reputable stove dealer is another source of advice on installing stoves. For more tips on safe stove installation, see page 91.

In order to choose the right stove for your heating needs, you should seek advice from people with experience in heating with wood. Local stove dealers are a good source. When shopping for stoves, take along a rough floor plan of the area you'll be heating. The plan should indicate room sizes, number and sizes of doors and windows, and where the stove will go. The efficiency of any stove will be affected by its location and by the flue pipe and chimney installation, as well as the way you use the stove.

Heat output

Most wood stoves are designed to heat one or two rooms only. If you're planning to use a stove to supplement your existing heating system or to heat a room addition or small cabin, you'll have to match the stove's heat output to the space you'll be heating. Should you decide to heat your entire house with wood, you may need several stoves, along with some type of fan or vent system to carry heat into outlying rooms. Or you may want to install a wood-burning furnace; some of these units are equipped to burn coal, fuel oil, or natural gas also.

Many stoves are rated according to the number of cubic feet of living space they'll heat. Basically, the figures tell you that one stove will throw out more heat than another. The amount of room space a stove will actually heat depends on a number of factors, including local climate, location of the stove, amount of insulation and weatherstripping in the house, and the kind and amount of wood burned with each firing. A knowledgeable stove dealer can help with information tailored to your needs.

Fuel efficiency

Though the amount of heat a stove produces is important, the amount of wood required to produce that heat is equally important—even more so if wood is expensive in your area. A stove's fuel efficiency is the percentage of wood's *potential* (stored) heat the stove converts into *useful* heat (that heat which

Wood stoves...the basic types

Potbelly stove

Barrel stove

Scandinavian stove

Circulating heater

Parlor stove

Range

Cookstove

Box stove

contributes to heating the living space). These percentages often appear in the literature provided by the stove manufacturer. If a stove is 60 percent efficient, it will produce twice as much heat with the same amount of wood as a stove that is only 30 percent efficient, all other things being equal.

Look for quality

Durability and ease of operation are two traits common to quality stoves. Some stoves built during the Victorian era are still in service today—testimony that a well-built stove will last a lifetime if properly cared for. Good stove designs, too, stand the test of time.

Stove construction. As with other appliances, the quality of both the work and the materials that go into a wood stove is important. Today, stoves are made of cast iron, plate steel, or a combination of the two.

Cast-iron stoves are made from separately cast plates, which are bolted together and their joints sealed with furnace cement to make them airtight. Eventually the cement will become brittle and fall out, and it must be replaced when it does. Cast iron is extremely hard and has a tendency to crack if the plates are cast too thin or the stove gets too hot.

The durability of a plate-steel stove depends on the thickness of the steel and the quality of the welds that hold it together. If the steel is too thin the stove may warp under extreme temperatures. A slight warp usually won't affect the performance of the stove, but it won't do much for the stove's looks. More serious warping may break the welds, causing the stove to lose its airtightness.

Both cast iron and steel are susceptible to corrosion from repeated firings. Of course, the thicker the material, the longer the stove will last. Many stoves have replaceable metal or firebrick linings that help prevent warping, cracking, and corroding.

Whether you're buying a new stove or an antique, check it carefully. Even new cast iron stoves may have cracks caused by improper casting or damage during shipping. On steel stoves, check all welds carefully for bubbles or cracks that may cause air leaks. On all stoves, make sure the loading door is properly aligned and seals tight against the stove body.

Some of the antiques you'll find may have tiny cracks; they can be repaired—patched with furnace cement. But if the cracks are large, the stove is virtually useless. Most old stoves will show some signs of corrosion inside the firebox; if the firebox walls are less than 1/16 inch thick, though, the old trooper is nearing the end of the trail.

Ease of operation

If you're planning to use your stove often, you'll appreciate one that's easy to use and requires little attention. The chores of refueling the stove and removing the ashes can become tedious, so before you buy a stove, find out how often these chores must be done.

Some stoves have the convenience of an ash removal pan to make unloading neat and easy. Otherwise you'll need a small ash shovel or ash rake and a metal ash bucket. Also, some stoves are easier to load than others. A large loading door is a plus—it allows larger pieces of wood to be burned and reduces the chances of your getting burned on the stove while loading. If the door is located near the bottom of the stove, there's less chance of smoke puffing into the room when you're feeding the fire, though you may have to get on your knees to load the wood unless the stove is placed on a raised hearth.

Quality stoves usually have insulated door handles. If yours doesn't, you'll have to keep a heavy glove handy for use once the stove gets hot.

Stove accessories

There are a number of devices on the market designed to increase the heat output of wood stoves. Called "heat extractors" or "heat exchangers," these devices are usually attached to the stovepipe to recapture warm air that would ordinarily be lost up the chimney. If you intend to buy one of these devices, check with your stove dealer to make sure the device you choose is compatible with your stove installation.

You'll also find devices for heating water. Some, like the heat exchangers, attach to the stovepipe; others are designed to fit inside or attach to the stove. Another device popular with wood-burning connoisseurs is the flue oven shown below.

Heat-recovery devices

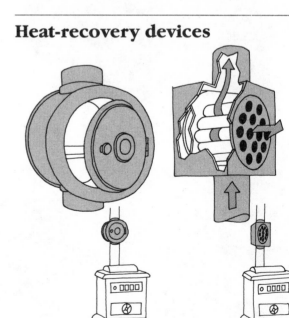

Add-on devices *such as flue oven (left) and fan-powered heat exchanger (right) help recover heat from flue.*

You'll find a variety of items available to aid in stove operation and maintenance. These include ash buckets and shovels; pokers, prongs, and bellows for tending the fire; and stove polish for cast iron stoves. However, devices or items that are absolutely essential to the stove's operation or installation—such as stovepipe, fireproofing materials, grates, and dampers—are not considered accessories and should be figured into the initial cost of the stove.

Safe installation & operation

Through their dependence on wood, our grandparents gained a healthy respect for fire and the damage it could do. The possibility of a stove-caused fire can be reduced to a minimum if you install the stove properly and use it safely.

Installing your stove

These are the three prime ingredients of a safe stove installation:

• *Adequate clearance.* Stove (unless it's a zero clearance stove) and stovepipe must be kept a safe distance from all combustible materials and surfaces.

• *Proper insulation.* Stovepipes must be insulated where they pass through walls, ceilings, and roof.

• *Wall and floor protection.* Combustible walls and floors near the stove must be covered with a noncombustible material such as asbestos board or masonry.

Typical stove clearances

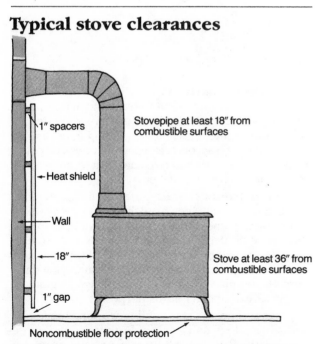

1" spacers

Stovepipe at least 18" from combustible surfaces

← Heat shield

← Wall

← 18" →

Stove at least 36" from combustible surfaces

1" gap

Noncombustible floor protection

Use these clearances for radiant stoves without listed clearance requirements; check local codes first.

Combustible walls or floors are defined as those containing wood, whether or not they're covered with a combustible material. To protect these surfaces, you can use masonry (brick, stone, ceramic tile) or a combination of sheet metal and asbestos board. The recommended thicknesses and installation of these materials will vary slightly according to local building codes. The drawing at right shows the minimum allowable clearances for the stove and stovepipe as set forth by the National Fire Protection Association. They're meant to be general guidelines only and may differ from clearances prescribed by the stove manufacturer or local building codes.

In addition, allow adequate clearance where the stovepipe enters the wall or ceiling (see drawing at left for these requirements).

Using your stove

Always follow the stove manufacturer's recommendations for safe stove operation. It's usually possible to burn a hotter fire than is recommended, but this is bad practice—frequent over-firing will decrease the stove's life and increase the possibility of disaster.

Most stoves require a breaking-in period. It's best to make the first few fires small, avoiding sudden bursts of heat. This will allow the stove to "season" slowly. At first, condensation will occur on the stove, and it should be wiped away so it doesn't stain the surface. If your stove is painted, it may "smell funny" in the beginning; this is only the oil in the paint evaporating—it will stop doing so after the first few fires.

Inspect the stovepipe occasionally to make sure all connections are tight. If you're continually burning small fires in the stove or using softwoods for fuel (see page 95), excess soot and creosote will build up in the stovepipe. Creosote, a flammable substance formed by tars and acids in the smoke, is the cause of chimney fires, and you should dismantle and check the stovepipe at least twice a year for creosote build-up if you use the stove regularly. There are chemical cleaners available for removing creosote from the stovepipe.

The stove itself should be checked now and then to make sure it is working properly. Some stove doors have asbestos gaskets that must be replaced occasionally. The damper in the stovepipe should also be working properly.

You should be prepared and know how to handle an emergency with your stove. If the fire gets too hot, you can control it by throwing several handfuls of baking soda on it; never douse the fire with water, because the sudden change in temperature may crack or warp the stove. And it's always a good idea to have a fire extinguisher handy, in case surrounding surfaces catch fire.

Always keep combustible materials (newspapers, furniture, wood, for example) away from the stove.

A FIRETENDER'S MANUAL

There's more to a cozy fire than just installing a fireplace. You'll have to find and store your fuel supply, and you may have to transport it yourself. You'll need some basic firetending tools and accessories to help you start and manage the fire and aid in cleanup after the flames have died down. And if you're counting on your fireplace to function as a heating source, you may want to install or employ some special heat-recovery and circulating devices. Finally, you'll need to add firebuilding techniques and fireplace and chimney maintenance procedures to your talents.

Even when the fireplace has been installed and is ready to use, the decisions continue: What will you burn? What accessories will you need? Will you expect the fireplace to help heat your home?

For fuel, wood is by far the favorite (see page 95)—affordable and widely available. Coal is long-burning and gives off an impressive amount of heat; you'll need a special grate to burn it. Composition logs, available at many supermarkets, are sometimes chemically treated to provide colorful flames and can burn for 2 to 3 hours; they are relatively expensive and should not be burned in combination with other fuels—to do so may be hazardous; follow the manufacturer's instructions carefully.

Finally, you can choose from a wide variety of fireplace accessories. Some are primarily decorative; others are functional. Heat-recovery devices that come in the form of add-on units should be on your list of accessories if you plan to use your fireplace to help heat the house. Even with a heat-efficient fireplace, these units further increase heat output.

Accessories for the fireside

Accessories fall into two categories. The first includes those that are highly useful for starting, managing, and cleaning up after the fire; these are often decorative as well, sometimes antique, adding interest to the fireside. The second category includes devices designed to recover and circulate heat to improve the fireplace's heating efficiency.

Functional and decorative items. To start the fire you can use a firelighter (usually decorative as well as functional), special long matches (available in a decorative holder), or a gas-fired log lighter. Grates or andirons will hold logs off the fireplace floor, and a screen or spark guard will help contain flying embers. (If you plan to burn coal, you'll need a grate specifically designed for this purpose.)

Tongs and pokers are useful in working the fire and moving logs, and a pair of leather welder's gloves can save the hair on the back of your hand when you're feeding the fire. To carry and hold a fuel supply you can use a canvas log carrier, a large basket, stoneware crock, log crib, or canvas and metal log carrier. For cleanup you'll find a shovel, broom, brush, ash hoe, and coal scuttle indispensable.

Standard fireplace tools are available in standing or wall-mounted sets that usually contain a shovel, poker, and a broom. For novelty or decoration you can add cooking accessories such as grills, pot hangers, and cauldrons.

Heat-saving devices

Though a crackling blaze in a conventional fireplace does much to warm the soul, it does surprisingly little to heat the room. Much of the heat from the fire goes up the chimney. In fact, convective currents from a fire in an open fireplace can actually pull warm air from the room and draw cold outside air into the house through cracks around doors and windows.

To increase heating efficiency, you must control the fire's burning rate, radiate or reflect heat back into the room, force warmed air back into the room by convection, or use a combination of these processes.

Optimum radiation grate. Resembling an ordinary grate, this device exposes more of the log's burning surface to the front of the fireplace, directing more radiant heat into the room.

Tempered glass screen. This screen, with adjustable air intakes, controls airflow into the fireplace, thus controlling the burning rate and allowing less warm room air to be sucked up the chimney.

Metal heat reflector. Heat normally absorbed by the back fireplace wall is reflected into the room by this metal sheet positioned behind the fire.

Convection grate. C-shaped tubes are fastened to a metal framework. When the tubes are heated, rising convective currents inside pull cool air into the bottom openings, expelling heated air through the top. A variation of this device uses a fan to force the air through the tubes, increasing efficiency.

Combining devices. An optimum radiation grate and a glass screen work well in tandem to boost radiant heat. Some devices combine a glass screen with a convection grate, with or without a fan-boost.

With a little ingenuity you can contrive your own heat-recovery system, using commercially available devices or inventing your own. When shopping for these devices, be sure you have the fireplace dimensions with you to assure a proper fit.

Using & maintaining the fireplace

Regardless of the type of fireplace, having an enjoyable fire will require some effort. Laying a good

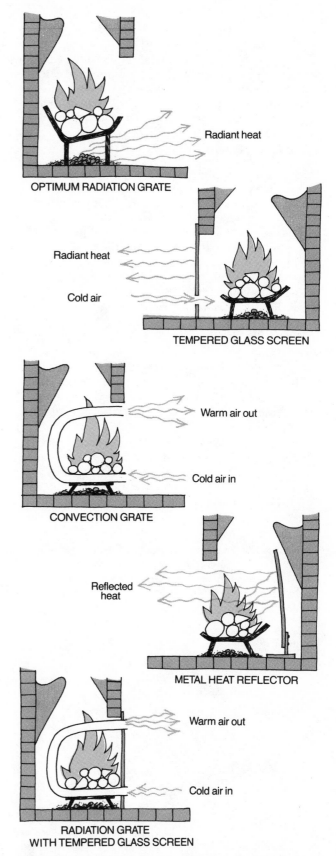

OPTIMUM RADIATION GRATE

Radiant heat

TEMPERED GLASS SCREEN

Radiant heat

Cold air

CONVECTION GRATE

Warm air out

Cold air in

METAL HEAT REFLECTOR

Reflected heat

RADIATION GRATE WITH TEMPERED GLASS SCREEN

Warm air out

Cold air in

Heat-recovery devices help save heat; arrows show how heat is directed into room by convection or radiation.

fire—one that starts easily and burns evenly—takes practice. With experience, you'll develop a knack for feeding the fire to maintain an even burning rate. The frequency of adding wood and the amount of wood required to keep the fire going vary with each fireplace design and depend on the kind and number of heat-recovery devices you use with your fireplace.

Laying a good fire

First, be sure the damper is open. (It's best to keep it closed between fires to minimize the heat loss from the house.) The logs should be laid on andirons or a fire grate to allow air to reach the fire from below. Without these, you'll have to use a pair of green logs to elevate the logs from the fireplace floor.

Next, put several crumpled or twisted sheets of newspaper in the center of the fireplace, then crisscross several sticks of kindling on top of the paper. Kindling can be any fast-burning wood split to one or two-finger width. Place three fairly small logs over the kindling, one on top of the other two, all with split sides down, since the split sides will catch faster than the bark sides.

The three logs confine the heat to the center of the fireplace, each radiating heat to the others. Don't stack these so tightly that the fire can't escape upward and burn evenly.

Just before lighting the fire, you can start a good updraft by holding a lighted twist of newspaper high in the throat of the fireplace. Then bring it down and use it to ignite the paper underneath the kindling.

If the fireplace lets smoke into the room, open a window so that the fire can draw more air to sustain an updraft.

Placing a large log at the back of the fire, with smaller logs toward the front, will help radiate the heat into the room. If the room tends to overheat, build a smaller fire behind a larger log placed near the front of the grate or andirons.

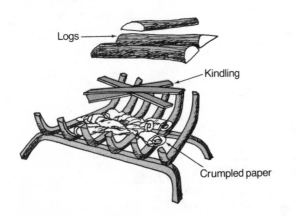

Logs

Kindling

Crumpled paper

The firescreen should remain closed unless you're watching the fire closely and are burning hardwood that won't throw sparks; it's always a good idea to keep a fire extinguisher nearby, too. Avoid frequent burning of paper and other burnable wastes, as this will fill the smoke shelf and flue with soot and creosote, necessitating more frequent cleaning.

Cures for a smoky fireplace

If your chimney installation meets all the requirements and still doesn't draw properly, you may need a special chimney cap. Surrounding hills or tall trees nearby can cause downdrafts that bring smoke into the room. A metal chimney cap—stationary or rotating—can cure the problem.

Forced air furnaces, kitchen fans, or doors opposite the fireplace opening can pull smoke from the fireplace into the room. Installing a solid room divider between the door and fireplace, turning the fans off, or installing a draft inducer (a fan that draws hot air up and out the flue) are possible remedies.

During spring, birds have been known to build nests in chimneys, a practice that—like beehives or drifting autumn leaves—can have smoky results. Check for such obstructions by lowering a light on an extension cord down the chimney. If there is no obstruction, and if the other possible causes of smoke have been eliminated, the problem could be faulty construction of the fireplace. In this case, a professional should be consulted. One possibility is that the fireplace opening could be too large for the flue area. If so, you might decrease the size of the opening—possibly by raising the hearth. An easier solution, and perhaps the best one, is to install a firebox insert, a prefabricated steel addition that slips into an existing firebox.

Cleaning the fireplace & chimney

Periodically, ashes will have to be removed from the fireplace. The bulk of this ash can be removed with a shovel. Avoid vigorous sweeping with a broom as this will send clouds of ash into the room. Remember, you can use the ash—it is rich in minerals and can be used in the garden as a nutrient, soil conditioner, or even a pest repellent.

Creosote. When moisture expelled from burning wood combines with combustible gases escaping unburned up the flue, creosote is formed. If layers of this messy, tarry substance are allowed to build up on the flue lining, the draft will be restricted and the creosote will bake on and become shiny. This deposit is highly flammable and can cause a chimney fire if not removed regularly. Fireplaces and stoves that send a lot of heat up the chimney will not produce much creosote; low flue temperatures, on the other hand, almost guarantee creosote deposits.

Frequent cleaning of the flue and chimney is the best remedy—once a year, at least, is a good idea.

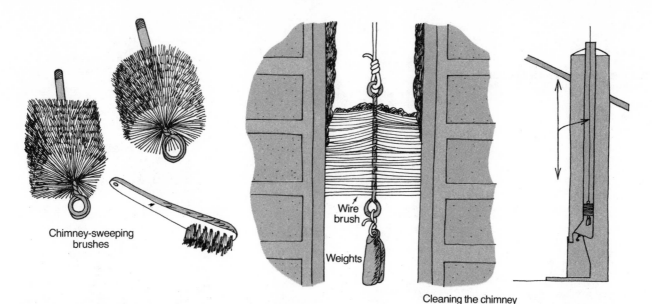

Cleaning the chimney

Chimney-sweeping brushes come in a variety of shapes and sizes. Upward movement (right) of brush scrapes off creosote; weights pull brush down again after each pass up flue.

Chimney cleaning. If you want to have the cleaning done, check the Yellow Pages under "Chimney Cleaning" to find a chimney sweep near you. If you choose to do the job yourself, here are a few tips:
• Use paper and masking tape to seal off the fireplace opening. Cover nearby furniture.
• Use a dust mask and goggles for protection.
• Use a good steel brush. Don't use chains, bags filled with rocks, or other heavy objects—they will damage your flue, and they don't do the job well.

To clean the flue, attach the brush to a rope at least the length of the flue and chimney. Attach weights (such as window sash weights) to the end of the brush (see drawing above). Pass the brush to the bottom of the flue and pull it up again. Repeat this operation until the brush no longer brings up large amounts of soot or creosote.

Flue pipes of wood stoves and freestanding fireplaces can be dismantled and cleaned outdoors.

Removing smoke stains. Smoke stains on masonry can be removed with a solution of 1/2 pound of trisodium-phosphate dissolved in a gallon of water. Wear gloves and apply with a scrub brush. For stubborn stains, muriatic acid will often do the job, but the acid may discolor brickwork and it should never be used on stone. The mixture should be one part acid to 10 parts water. Mix the solution in a wide-mouthed jar, pouring the water in first, then adding the acid. Apply with a cloth and immediately rinse with water.

Wood to burn

Woods fall into two general categories—hardwoods and softwoods. Hardwoods include all species of broad-leafed, usually deciduous, trees like the oak,

hickory, and maple. Softwoods include the conifers and other needle-leafed evergreens such as pine, fir, and cedar.

Hardwoods are generally denser and less resinous than softwoods and burn more slowly. Softwoods burn hot and fast and make excellent kindling.

Species within these two categories have individual characteristics worth considering. For example, straight-grained woods such as birch or red oak are easier to split than woods with a spiral or twined grain pattern. Hardhack, or ironwood, lives up to its name and can quickly dull a blade or ax bit. Many softwoods are smoke producers; others contain moisture pockets causing them to pop and throw off sparks as they burn. Because of their high resin (sap) content, softwoods produce more creosote, which means more frequent flue and chimney cleaning (see above).

Among the best firewoods, experienced wood burners generally agree, are ash, beech, birch, hickory, oak, and hard maple. These have high heat values, burn well, produce little smoke, and split fairly easily.

Regardless of the variety of the wood, it is best not to burn it unless it's seasoned (air-dried). Also, wood that is seasoned weighs less, is easier to handle, ignites faster, burns better, and produces less soot and creosote. Ideally, firewood for winter should have been cut during the preceding winter or spring and allowed to season during the summer and fall.

For proper seasoning, stack wood off the ground on parallel poles or stringers or rows of concrete blocks. Use either the parallel or crisscross method of stacking. The former is more compact; the latter allows better air circulation, which speeds up seasoning. Pieces with bark should be placed on top, bark side up. Stacks higher than 3 feet should have braces.

Index

Photographers

Edward B. Bigelow: 17, 20 top, 58 left, 59 top left & right, 60 right, 61 bottom, back cover top left. **Jack McDowell:** 18, 19, 20 bottom, 22 bottom left & right, 23, 27 top, 31 top left & right, 32 top, 32 bottom left, 33 top, 34 top, 35 bottom, 36, 37, 38, 39 top, 42 top, 47 bottom, 50, 51, 52 bottom, 53, 54 bottom, 55 bottom, 56 bottom, 59 bottom, 60 left, 61 top, 62 bottom, 63 top, 63 bottom right, back cover bottom. **Steve W. Marley:** front cover, 21 top, 24, 25, 26 , 27 bottom, 28 top, 30, 31 bottom, 32 bottom right, 33 bottom, 34 bottom, 35 top, 39 bottom left & right, 41, 42 bottom, 43, 44, 45, 46, 48 49, 52 top, 55 top left & right, 56 top, 57, 62 top, 63 left. **Jim Peck:** 21 bottom, 22 top, 28 bottom, 29, 54 top. **Rob Super:** 47 top left & right, 58 right, back cover top right. **Darrow M. Watt:** 40.